SHE WROTE THE SONGS

Born on Canada's West Coast, Patricia Hammond moved to the UK in 2001. She has forged a versatile career as a singer, performing opera in Athens and Wexford, oratorio throughout Europe, and ragtime in a 1911 battle bus at the London Transport Museum. In November 2018 she sang 1918's 'The Rose of No Man's Land' in the Bundestag in Berlin for the German commemoration of the end of the First World War, for guests including Angela Merkel and Emmanuel Macron. Her recordings are played on radio stations around the world. She can be heard and (just) seen in the film *Tolkien*.

She has written for *Telegraph Magazine*, *The Lancet Psychiatry* and the *Mail on Sunday*. From 2013 to 2017, she wrote a music column for *Chap*, a vintage lifestyle magazine.

She Wrote the Songs

PATRICIA HAMMOND

Valley Press

First published in 2020 by Valley Press
Woodend, The Crescent, Scarborough, YO11 2PW
www.valleypressuk.com

First edition, first printing (July 2020)

ISBN 978-1-908853-58-5
Cat. no. VP0116

Copyright © Patricia Hammond 2020

The right of Patricia Hammond to be identified as the author of this work has been asserted in accordance with the Copyright, Designs and Patents Act 1988.

All rights reserved. No part of this publication may be reproduced, stored in or introduced into a retrieval system, or transmitted in any form, by any means (electronic, mechanical, photocopying, recording or otherwise) without prior written permission from the rights holders.

A CIP record for this book is available from the British Library.

Cover design by Fitzpatrick Design.
Text design and editing by Jo Haywood.

Printed and bound in Great Britain by
TJ International Ltd, Padstow, Cornwall.

Contents

A Song to Sing 9
A Very Large House 16
Claribel and the Beethoven Lens 24
Folk Music Suffrage 35
Children, Church, Change 49
Songs as Gifts 58
Two Identities in South London 66
The Refuge and Reform of Caroline Sheridan Norton 81
India By Way of a Parlour Piano (and the North Circular) 91
Something Other 100
The Use of it All 111

References 117
Bibliography 121
Track List 125

Acknowledgements

Kelley Swain for being my writing companion and for introducing me to Valley Press.

Andrea Vargas Kmecova for her willingness to be involved in this project and, vitally, playing the piano and putting up with rehearsals.

Janice and Bill Rossen for encouragement and so generously sponsoring the making of the CD.

Jen Passmore for reading this and asking crucial questions.

Valerie Flessati for proofreading and thought-provoking discussions.

Felicity Manning for reading this and telling me it was good!

My parents for letting their children grow up in a house filled with old books and clutter.

Ian Grieve for vital assistance with Australian magazine archives and Old Time Radio.

Andrea Tanner for her support and help with ancestry resources.

Wallace Kwong at the British Library for tracking down "La Belle Assemblee".

Karen Rekla for enthusiasm and insisting I should make some illustrations.

Paul Dashwood for welcoming me so warmly, opening up his family archive and talking about his grandmother, Avril Coleridge-Taylor.

Timothy Dilke for welcoming us into his house, talking about his grandmother, Ethel Clifford, and having us perform a concert in his parlour.

Fiona Mariah for finding (and paying for!) the music for "The Wide Brown Land" in Australia.

Eva Gersbach and the Gersbach family for inspiration, encouragement, and Helen.

Carina Roter for general fabulousness.

for Sweetface

A Song to Sing

A COUPLE OF decades ago, the *Vancouver Sun* ran a piece entitled "Your trash is her treasure" about an eccentric nine-year-old who collected beer bottle caps and old sheet music.

I would have preferred to collect antique paintings and jewellery, but being poor, I chose something people gave away for free. It worked; amused adults opened their basements and attics to me. And on the rare occasions I saw bottle caps or sheet music in shops, prices were in line with what a girl could earn from neighbours by watering plants and feeding cats.

I grew to love my collections. Designs from the tops of bottles took me to other countries and other eras. A man with a big moustache wearing a homburg and holding a tankard of ale made me think of mountains and loud wooden taverns, a clear icy moon shining on blue snow. And a woman in an enormous pink hat on the cover of a piece of sheet music from 1904, sitting under a tree, white blouse billowing from a tiny waist with meadows in the background, took me to fairyland. Actually, it was better than fairyland. In addition to her beauty, she had all the reality and vividness of the man on the beer bottle cap. She lived because she sang. She sang because when I turned her over, there was music inside.

The smell of stale beer was evocative, but sheet music had eclipsed bottle caps completely by the time I was eleven. There was a lot of it about; a mere seventy years earlier, every major department store had a sheet music department, in addition to the individual music shops on the street. Records at the time were still scratchy novelties providing a crude rhythm to dance to, or the faint glimmer of a famous opera singer's voice, thus music in the home was mostly music one made oneself. Every week, new songs would come in, publishers vying with each other in their cover designs to attract the eyes of the undecided. These covers were what I cared about most at the beginning but, as my piano skills improved, I was able to pay more attention to the music. Soon I didn't mind so much whether they were illustrated or not, so long as I liked what I played.

I found most of it tuneful and human, not as abstract as dear old Bach's preludes or Czerny's studies in the solid music-study books. Songs in fluttery old sheet music got their effect quickly. The melodies were clear, the emotions in the lyrics were direct, and I found myself humming them as I went to school. Songs about gardens, songs that longed for a lost home, songs about walking by the sea. Emotional ballads, clear-eyed waltzes, foxtrots that gave me a more confident gait.

I brought some of these pieces of sheet music to my piano teacher. She dismissed them with the sweeping word "schmaltz". I asked my mother what that meant. "Sentimental." I still didn't understand. I knew that the songs were from a bygone age, certainly a more sentimental one, but that made them all the more valuable to me. Meanwhile, I started to notice a near-absence of women in the Royal Conservatory of Music graded piano syllabus, even though there were loads of women composers and lyricists in my sheet music collection. I wondered, as I grew in cynicism and looked around me, if there was a connection between the dismissal of the music in my sheet music collection, and this preponderance of women?

I passed my piano exams by playing the prescribed, serious pieces in the books, but kept up the illicit practise of what I'd been told were called "parlour songs". Music for the home. Home-played. Down-to-earth in their technical requirements, like chocolate chip cookies. Music lessons, on the other hand, seemed bent on working me slowly towards a Cordon Bleu Diplôme de Pâtisserie. And yet, every cordon bleu chef ought, surely, to be able to make amazing chocolate chip cookies?

I brought a nice big bag of sheet music with me when I moved to Vancouver to go to Music College. "Parlour songs!" the music history teacher laughed, then became serious and shook his head. "They're only fit for a domestic setting."

"These songs are for amateurs to sing," my singing teacher said.

Puzzled, I compared Carrie Jacobs-Bond's "A Perfect Day" *(CD track 10)* with Giordani's "Caro Mio Ben", a song every voice teacher had their students learn and perfect. They were equally playable, equally accessible – actually, Jacobs-Bond's song was better for me as a young singer because its rising phrase brought my easier, lower voice into the upper part that tended to weaken and grow hoarse. Giordani was a Neapolitan composer of operas mostly, with a career that took in Austria, Germany, the Netherlands, France, England and Ireland. Jacobs-Bond was an American single mother who wrote songs to support herself and her son. One song was of unrequited love, and the other, of happy friendship.

Slowly it became apparent that for songs to be taken seriously, the composers had to be famous, usually through having created something big, and the poems would be, preferably, by famous poets. The subject matter was dramatic, universal. About dying, or one-sided love, for example, or, like Goethe's poem about the trout in the stream or the rose in the hedge, symbolic of something universal – in these cases, seduction. The subject matter for parlour song seemed too small or trivial for the professors.

I tried to interest the teachers in the melodious, clever, richly evocative music of Liza Lehmann, considered an "art song" composer in her day, highbrow enough to have been a professor at the Guildhall School of Music, and the first president of the Society of Women Musicians. "Liza Lehmann didn't write any large-scale works," the history teacher said. Neither did Henri Duparc or Roger Quilter, I protested, but their handful of songs had brought them fame and respect in their own day and in ours, and many students were encouraged to include Duparc and Quilter in their final recitals. These arguments were not sticking.

In my tiny rented room in the evenings, I read Virginia Woolf's words:

"This is an important book, the critic assumes, because it deals with war. This is an insignificant book, because it deals with the feelings of women in a drawing-room." [1]

It was true that Liza Lehmann's first big success, *In A Persian Garden,* had its premiere in a drawing room. Was the taint of the drawing room so deadly as to banish a composer from the list of standard works?

I raged that the songs written by Liza Lehmann, Teresa del Riego, May Brahe and Amy Woodforde-Finden were dismissed so quickly.

They may have written for a market of ladies who played and sang at the parlour upright, sheet music kept neatly in the piano bench when not in use, or traded with friends like cake recipes, but what were madrigals if not domestic music? And we studied madrigals in music history. The College Singers, made up of the best voices in the school, sang many of these sixteenth century ditties in formal settings to a church-like silence of veneration. Despite the fact they were created to be sung amidst dishes of half-finished sauces and scraps of roasted meat, wine glass in hand, as Renaissance composer Thomas Morley made clear in 1597: "Supper being ended, and Musicke books, according to the custome being brought to the table: the mistresse of the house presented mee with a part, earnestly requesting mee to sing."[2]

So, even my theory of habitat destruction didn't stand up. People no longer gathered around the parlour piano to listen to each other singing songs, but neither did we sing in four parts after a banquet. Madrigals could survive out of context, so why couldn't parlour songs?

The crazy answer was that they *did* survive out of context. People loved them in recitals. I'd sneak them in, and a song like "Bless This House" would always bring down the house.

I still had hopes of finding a habitat for parlour song somewhere in the world. My sheet music collection, like my beer bottle cap collection before it, had taken me not only to the past, but to other countries, which I was determined to see for myself. Europe looked full of old nooks and ancient crannies, and I thought that around some of those, my songs could thrive. Continuing to collect sheet music in bookshops, friends' piano benches, charity shops and library sales, I carefully saved my earnings until I had enough for a ticket to Europe.

Once there, I found that the museums and the historic architecture housed disconcertingly modern people. Audiences still loved the songs, but those in control of what went into concert series were another matter. When singing for one of London music's arbiters of taste, a coach at the Royal Opera House, I pulled out a few pieces of old music for him to look at. "Good Lord," he said. I persisted, explaining what I saw in the songs, and what audiences seemed to see in them. "Well," he shrugged, "Charlotte Church seems to have a career singing all manner of rubbish."

Just holding up the title page of May H Brahe's "Bless This House" was enough to send an auditioning panel into a storm of titters. "Harry Secombe used to sing that one as a joke," said a man on the Royal Overseas League's judging table, causing a second ripple of mirth. I doubt he would have giggled at the estimable Boosey & Co, publisher of Elgar, Rossini, Verdi, Bartok, Britten and Vaughan Williams, who saw fit to keep Mrs. Brahe on a yearly retainer in exchange for any songs she decided to present them with. Only a tiny handful of other composers were accorded that honour at the time, and one of them was Igor Stravinsky.

What is it about a house that makes people laugh? Are we not supposed to sing about them?

To be fair, people sometimes laugh at Bach's *Coffee Cantata* and Richard Strauss's *Sinfonia Domestica* as well. But the reputations of these two estimable gentlemen lie in organ lofts and cathedrals, symphonic halls and opera houses – not private houses.

And if these women composers' lives are veiled in obscurity or contempt, what of the women whose verses they set? Take Helen Taylor, frequent collaborator of Boosey & Hawkes' valued Ms Brahe. Her words were framed and hung on the walls of Eisenhower's White House, yet she is described fleetingly, and inaccurately, as "a governess" in the few books that bother to mention her and I had to go through gravestones on an ancestry database in an attempt to find her. Of Constance Morgan, nothing exists save for a dusty old book called *The Song of a Tramp, and Other Poems*. Researching her is like looking up one's family tree, but with fewer clues.

I often see an air of amused indulgence given to this genre, as if a subject matter dealing with gentle, sweet things, melancholy rather than tragedy, is somehow weak. But there is a story of survival behind the songs, which I found empowering. These women did more than write about domestic settings. With their writing, both music and verse, they earned the money to guarantee their own domestic security. Carrie Jacobs-Bond, who wrote "A Perfect Day", was widowed and crippled and unable to pay her rent when she formed her own music publishing company at the age of 33. Despite all major publishers rejecting her songs as either too highbrow or not highbrow enough, they became enormously popular, and she published 200 of them between 1896 and her death in 1946. In all, she sold 20 million copies of sheet music. The poet Josephine Peabody was first published in *The Woman's Journal* in 1883, when she was 14. Her family was living in poverty in Brooklyn after the death of her father, and her verses provided crucial income. Her poem "The House and the Road" *(CD track 1)* beautifully sums up a dilemma that many women and girls must have felt in the 1890s, when secretarial and other clerical jobs were opening up for them.

Apart from musical merit, these poems and songs offer an alternative narrative for historians. Sitting silently in archives the world over is a subtly nuanced variety of subject-matter embracing not just the domestic, but the exotic, the childlike, the mystical and the gothic, asking questions about grief and identity, such as Minnie Aumonier's "Can Sorrow Find Me," *(CD track 24)* which spoke so strongly to Avril Coleridge-Taylor as she struggled to find her way as a woman of colour who wanted to write ballets and conduct symphonies.

History is often like the news: if it bleeds, it leads. A diffuse and subtle message tends to be shunted into footnotes. The story of women's suffrage is usually told in a series of violent snapshots that includes women chained to Downing Street railings, force-feedings in Holloway prison and Emily Wilding Davison's martyrdom. We rarely learn of Mary Neal's Espérance working-girls' club, singing folk songs and dancing the Morris at Suffrage events. Students of nineteenth century British political reform know about Caroline Norton's tireless lobbying for married women to have the right to own property but are usually unaware of her large circle of supportive female friends, and the compelling solidarity of their sad songs.

Whether these women wrote songs because they were a comfort, or found themselves barred from positions at cathedrals and universities where they might have experimented with larger forms; whether they were forced to write their era's most commercial type of music because of financial necessity, or simply loved songs more than any other type of music, they all have a story to tell, a song to sing.

Poet Josephine Peabody was first published in The Woman's Journal in 1883 at the age of 14. Her verses supported her family after the death of her father.

A Very Large House

May Brahe had the honour of being one of the small handful of composers Boosey & Hawkes chose to put on an annual retainer. "Bless This House" was by far her most famous work, though as a sheet music collector I also came across as many copies of "I Passed By Your Window" and "It's Quiet Down Here". Her name was very, very familiar to me, surfacing in piano benches, sheet music collections bound in hard leather covers to protect them, or tattered and flaking, loose amongst cardigan knitting patterns, thrice-tested recipes from 1930s *Chatelaine* magazines, in boxes under pianos, in plastic bags given to me from neighbours whose musical grandmothers had died. Wherever sheet music was found, May Brahe was there.

To research this chapter I went first to the enormous wall of reference books in the rare books and music reading room at the British Library, and headed for the Encyclopedia Britannica of music, the *Grove Dictionary*. But in the 29-volume *New Grove*, the Stanley Sadie edition, there was nothing between Braham and Brahms. That wasn't too surprising. Very often, despite its larger size, the *New Grove* leaves out the composers I tend to be interested in. By Sadie's time, what was popular fifty or sixty years earlier was deemed old-fashioned as lofty academics tried to reshuffle history. So, I went to the Eric Blom edition of 1927, but again found nothing between Regency tenor John Braham, strutting in his musketeer boots and sword, and Johannes Brahms' paunch and whiskers.

Might it be considered pop music? I crouched to pull out the vast breezeblock of the *Guinness Encyclopedia of Popular Music*, and … nothing between Billy Bragg and Daryl Braithwaite. Next on the shelf was *Old English Popular Music*. Far too early; old in that book meant 1600s. So, narrowing things down, an encyclopedia of modern British composers. Nothing between Arthur Bliss and Benjamin Britten. A dictionary of silent cinema music? Braham and Brahms again. Only, this Braham wrote "Dancing Honeymoon". And anyway, "Bless This House" is from 1927, the tail end of silent cinema. Surely, she'd be in Gene Claghorn's *Women Composers and Songwriters*. Even if she's not considered a composer in the old-fashioned sense, she certainly was a songwriter. I went to a British Library terminal and ordered it. An hour later, I collected it from the desk and set off back to desk 292. But before I reached it, I'd found she hadn't been included. I snorted in disgust and took it back to the counter before having one last look at the encyclopedia wall.

Finally, in *Popular Music 1920-1979, A Revised Cumulation of 18,000 American Popular Songs* published by the Gale Research Company, there she was. May H Brahe, "Bless This House". No more. The two names kind enough to make a space for her between them were the silent-film Braham, Philip, composer of not just "Dancing Honeymoon" but also "Limehouse Blues", and Jerome Brailey "Tear the Roof off the Sucker (Give Up the Funk)".

It turned out that the place to find out about May H Brahe wasn't in reference books, but in old periodicals, themselves as ephemeral as sheet music. *Women's Weekly, Woman's Day and Home, Woman's World, Ladies' Home Journal*. May's story is told alongside full instructions "for knitting a new-style bolero, and … a bargain pattern offered of a tailored shirt-waist dress for the fuller figure". The biographical pieces themselves celebrate the chintz on Brahe's furniture, containing phrases like "May Brahe, dislodging a kitten from her favourite armchair in the sun … " and quoting time and again her claim that "I have composed many of my best works at the kitchen sink". In the year of her death, she was even to be seen in an advert for Lipton Tea.

She also composed so prolifically she had to use pseudonyms to get it all published. Born Mary Hannah Dickson, she was, variously, Donald Crichton, Stanley Dickson ("Thanks Be To God", one of her best-sellers*)*, Stanton Douglas, Wilbur B Fox, Henry Lovell, Eric Faulkner, Mervyn Banks, Mary Brahe, Mary Hannah Morgan and Alison Dodd. And for her foray into music hall territory, she was George Pointer, in a song called "I Don't Know How I'm Going to Wait Till Sunday".

Her story ought to have a familiar ring to all students of female composers from that time: her mother died when she was twelve, and her father's business – cordial manufacture – began to fail when she

May H Brahe's story is told in periodicals — Woman's Weekly, Woman's Day and Home, Woman's World, Ladies' Home Journal — rather than reference books.

was fifteen, so she left school to teach piano, started accompanying singers and soon was writing songs for the singers to perform. But crucially, I didn't know that day at the British Library to look in an Australian composers encyclopedia. As it happened, Boosey & Hawkes' star songwriter had been born in East Melbourne.

In 1912, at the age of 27, she took a huge chance and paid seventeen Australian pounds for a single passage to London. She left her husband and two little boys behind and, earning tuppence for each sheet of music sold, composed at as fast a rate as she could, and played the piano at Terry's Silent Cinema on the Strand until she could afford to bring her family over in 1914. That same year, she had a daughter. Her husband, Carl Frederick Brahe, enlisted, then came back from the war in 1919 only to die in a motor accident. On a trip to Southend, according to the *Southend Times*, she saw light singer and comedian George Albert Morgan, then part of a concert party, perform one of her songs. It was "love at first sight", gushed newspapers from Bath to Belfast. They married secretly at a Paddington Register office in 1922 and added another child to the three she had already. The family lived in St John's Wood, in a large house on the High Street. It was there she wrote "Bless This House".

Old newspapers as well as old magazines are full of Mrs Brahe's pieces. Going to the newspaper archives to see where her songs were performed is like falling into a large warm vat of tea and crumpets. "The Mayoress At Home", "Helping the building fund", "A Garden Programme", "Concert in a church", "Pleasant Evening for Gowers Green Primrose Leaguers", "Proceeds for the Organ". May Brahe's songs in Women's Institute meetings, opera at Nether Stowey, the Bath Orpheus Glee Society, the Boyscouts' Camping Fund in North Devon, vocal recitals in West Hartlepool; Tableaux Vivants – Entertainment for the General Hospital and Blue Cross in Cheltenham, the Mothers' Union in Rochdale, Social Hours in Methodist churches, "Wireless Whispers"; performances by the Gresham Singers, Miss Gladys Harris "The Cornish Blackbird", and even the Alpha Male Voice Choir in Antrim. One advert, in a margin, suggests buying some May Brahe songs "For yourself or your friends". Very often her songs are singled out amongst others for getting the most reaction from the audience, and of particularly suiting the singer: Miss Jackson "elicited enthusiastic applause for her sweet and expressive rendering" of "It's Quiet Down Here" in 1925. Phrases crop up: "suited the singer well ... wonderful tendresse"; "And a less sombre note"; and "some idea of the beauty of the music will be gained from the fact that the composer was May Brahe". A 1935 article, "A Song That Brought Romance", told of Brahe's "Meadow Sweet", which dramatic contralto Dorothy Clark sang on the BBC, causing a young man to fall in love, court and marry her. The wisdom of writing under pseudonyms is proven in a few listings where she's represented twice at a recital, such as the Enoch Concerts in London's Methodist Central Hall in 1923. Besides singing some of Stanley Dickson's ballads, Miss Clara Serena "introduced with success the fourth and last novelty of the day, a Northern Lament" by Mrs May Brahe. Who, of course, was also Stanley Dickson.

Brahe's world is a busy, friendly one, of fundraising, wives and mothers and villages, a picture of human proportions. May Brahe didn't just write for domestic music-making; she championed it. She called it "music for music's sake" and spoke at women's clubs on the subject. She liked to tell of the time when singing professor Albert Visetti gave her a tour of the Royal College of Music. Shocked at how many students teemed its hallways and practise rooms, "I expressed surprise and said to him, 'Surely they are not all going to be professional?'. 'Oh no,' he said, 'fortunately the dear young ladies will most of them get married'." After the anecdote, she continued, "And that is the real point: professionalism is far from being the only aspect of music. They can give intense pleasure to their own circle and, most of all, can have a source of solace and enjoyment, which is an everlasting delight."[1] And there was May, seeing the inside of a music school for the very first time, but respected so highly in the music world that the great Visetti was hosting her for lunch. She herself had been taught by three ladies in Australia: Emily Dare for piano, Alice Rebottaro for voice and Mona McBurney for counterpoint and harmony. In 1954, she told an interviewer that she wrote her first proper song as a schoolgirl to lyrics by Sappho. Crucially, it was her mother who started her writing music – Scottish-born singer Margaret Dickson, trained in England and Europe, who made up songs for her children, seated at the piano. May said: "I just naturally followed suit".

In 1920s and 30s Britain, May Brahe was celebrated on radio, as well as making a variety of personal appearances, including one at the Ideal Homes Exhibition in Southampton alongside Evelyn Hardy's London Ladies Band, which performed popular music in scarlet costumes and white wigs, according to the *Era* magazine in May 1930, "attracting enormous crowds." May played the piano as Evelyn Hardy's celebrated cornet provided the melody lines for Brahe's best-known songs.

Then, in 1939, she moved back to Australia "for the duration", she told the newspapers. In October of that year, a reporter for the *Sydney Sun* wrote "She feels that her latest work, 'A Prayer for Peace', in view of the war situation, has failed in its purpose". She made it clear to the press that she did not intend to write any war songs, but shortly after, amidst the destruction of churches, hospitals and entire cities, her ballads had a strong resurgence. "Bless This House" *(CD track 2)* sold 90,000 copies in 1943 alone. Her hymn to the hearth had become a prayer. That same year, Helen Taylor, who had written the words for it, died suddenly in London, her story lost amidst countless other tragedies. She'd not only written dozens of texts for Brahe, but also Easthope Martin's famous "Come to the Fair" and lyrics for songs by Granville Bantock ("Silent Strings"), Cecil Armstrong Gibbs ("Requiescat") and Michael Head ("Come Take Your Lute"). Brahe spoke to the newspapers again to dispel melodramatic rumours that her friend had died in poverty. No, she said, Helen Jane Taylor "earned £1,000 a year from her lyrics."

May spoke at women's clubs in Australia, wrote more songs, was celebrated at "Feminist Club" luncheons and gave pragmatic and perhaps unappreciated advice to the Australian Parliamentary Standing Committee on Broadcasting in 1950, telling them not to label music as Australian, because it would be taken as a derogatory term. I reckon this to be a telling insight into her thirty years spent in England.

While "Bless This House" was a song for soirees and fundraisers for the Mothers' Union, a prayer for a safe haven amidst falling bombs, I believe that the reason I found a listing for "May Brahe: Bless This House" in an encyclopedia published in Michigan, and not London, is because in America "Bless This House" doesn't mean just any old house.

When Mamie Eisenhower came to the White House in 1953, she brought a plaque of Helen Taylor's poem with her and hung it up in a prominent location. She'd also placed it on the wall in the Eisenhowers' twenty-eight previous residences. At her husband's inauguration ceremony, Gladys Swarthout had sung Brahe's song to the multitude. When the Eisenhowers retired, Mamie put up *two* plaques of the poem on their front door in Gettysburg. In

2005, George W Bush had Susan Graham perform "Bless This House" for his inauguration, perhaps as a response to 9/11. It had also been performed at the funeral of Franklin D Roosevelt on April 14th 1945.

A lifetime before Helen Taylor or May Brahe had put pen to paper, John Adams, the first president to live in the White House, wrote a prayer in a letter to his wife on November 2nd 1800. "I pray Heaven to bestow the best of blessings on this house and all that shall hereafter inhabit it. May none but honest and wise men ever rule under this roof."[2] FDR had that engraved into the mantelpiece in the state dining room. Just to make sure.

America isn't ruled by a castle; it is ruled by a house which is an echo of the millions of houses that voted for its current inhabitants. *Good Housekeeping* compares presidential candidates' wives' cookie recipes, for heaven's sake. The pursuit of happiness and the cult of domesticity are intertwined, and Franklin D Roosevelt knew this well when he opted to broadcast his "Fireside Chats". In March 1933, the USA was on the brink of disaster as financial panic set in and millions of people were set to withdraw their money from the banks and plunge the country into chaos. For the first time, a president chose not to orate but to speak calmly and directly via radio, as if he was sitting in the listener's living room. "My friends," he began. According to May Brahe in an interview with the *Sydney Morning Herald* in October 1954, Roosevelt opened these Fireside Chats – or as she called them "armchair chats" – with a recording of "Bless This House." The populace remained calm and the Fireside Chats became an institution.

Compare England's favourite performance of "Bless This House", given by Gracie Fields in 1950, with Mahalia Jackson's version six years later, and we have the difference between something intimate and something of epic proportions – a towering anthem to a house that rules all houses.

For me as a singer, it's an unassuming song on paper that enters into another league when presented to an audience. It always has a greater effect than I expect: rapt silence and an almost startling focus from all the eyes in the room. As a renter unlikely ever to afford a house of my own, I find a periodic reacquainting with Laura Ingalls

Wilder's *Little House* books helpful in understanding the precious sacredness of a house that is truly yours, a pride in every scrubbed board, and handmade patchwork quilts that represent happy, quiet evenings with loved ones. That, and singing "Bless This House".

There is no commemorative blue plaque on the house in St John's Wood where May Brahe wrote the song. But perhaps her loyalties were not, ultimately, with a house at all. In 1949, Boosey's Australia published her setting of Dorothea MacKellar's poem "A Wide Brown Land For Me" *(CD track 3)*. It wasn't published anywhere else.

Claribel and the Beethoven Lens

The rain fell madly, and the wind
Came driving from the sea;
'God save the souls upon the deep
This awful night!' saith she.

from "A Storm" by Charlotte Alington Barnard[1]

IN MUSIC COLLEGE, I had to scrape together $50 of cat-sitting earnings for Donald J Grout's *A History of Western Music*. At the time, I didn't pay much attention to the very first word of the title.

As I flipped through it on a bench under the trees, using the smell of new textbook to take the edge off the loss of my fifty bucks, I realised that I'd spent all this money on a long, long book on Beethoven. It seemed that the bulk of it was three thick chapters on, respectively, early Beethoven, middle Beethoven and late Beethoven. With a bit of "before" Beethoven and a bit of "after" Beethoven on either side.

It seemed that every other part of western music had to be seen through Beethoven-glasses. Who wrote string quartets? Who wrote symphonies? Who wrote choral works? Who wrote an opera or two? The composers who could mark all these on their bingo card were in; worthy of study. Continuing with the Beethoven-lens, if a composer was angsty, pushed against convention and bent the trends of these forms, then – hooray! – they were even more worthy. So, instead of looking at composers who were creating interesting and beautiful music in the 1910s and 20s like Schulhoff, Zemlinsky, Smyth, Martinu, Villiers Stanford and Bliss, we had to focus on Berg, Webern and Schoenberg, because Berg, Webern and Schoenberg were doing something different that pissed people off, like Beethoven did in his day. At least, that's how I saw it, under those trees.

The other thing I noticed, aside from the Beethoven-lens, was the persistent notion that, in an overview of western music history, we should abandon England after poor Purcell died of his chill in 1695, only coming back for Benjamin Britten in the 1940s. So, for two hundred and forty years, not a heck of a lot happened, except maybe some Elgar, who is introduced in the sub-category of Nationalism, what Smetana was for the Czechs.

I often heard people smugly, knowingly, quote the phrase "Das Land ohne Musik" ("The Land Without Music"), when speaking of Britain. Even pre-internet, it didn't take me too long to find out where the phrase came from: a German music critic in 1904. *Das Land ohne Musik* was the title of his book. Oskar Adolf Hermann Schmitz was a keen astrologist, fascinated by the themes of sadism, religion, psychoanalysis, Satanism and the erotic, as well as the tastes of the English. In a varied oeuvre, two years before *Das Land Ohne Musik* he published a book called *Haschisch*. But returning to the former, he wrote: "The English are the only cultured nation without its own music (except street music)."[2] Then he goes on to say that this means that the Englishman's life is poorer as a result, because even the littlest music allows one to bear misfortunes by losing oneself, to resolve one's troubles, in harmony. (I guess if that fails, there's always hashish.)

It was, ironically, precisely in this activity, "*noch so wenig*", (even so little) that the English *were* resolving their problems in harmony, in two rich musical streams. For all his bohemian unconventionality, Oskar had the Beethoven glasses firmly fixed to his head. Sure, in those two hundred and forty years, Britain's opera houses were unabashedly dependent on the Italian and German composers, but not everything takes place in opera houses. Up and down Pall Mall, in Holborn, the Square Mile and in all the major towns of the land, groups of men were fully occupied in their supper clubs, composing and singing "glees" and "catches" in four-parts. And in the parlours at home, at upright pianos, box pianos, harmoniums and baby grands, women were singing their very own little songs.

Very recently, little songs have been sufficient to pave the way to greatness, particularly for pop musicians. And every time I hear social commentators or music critics refer to, say, Burt Bacharach or Paul McCartney as "great composers", I think of Claribel.

Composers always had a first name, often a middle name, a last name and a set of dates in my piano books. Though the first time I saw "Wolfgang Amadeus Mozart (1756-1791)", I thought it was his phone number. In the popular sheet music I collected, often there was a team of songwriters: "My Sin Was Loving You" was by Buddy De Sylva, Lew Brown and Ray Henderson. So, when I saw the single word "Claribel" at the top of some of the songs, I didn't think it was a composer's name. I wasn't sure what it was.

And I kept seeing it. Again and again. "Take Back the Heart" *(CD track 4)* was my favourite. I had four different copies of this song, each from a different publisher. Sometimes "Claribel" was in the upper left, sometimes the upper right, sometimes it was not there at all and sometimes it was replaced with the name of an arranger, in the conventional male-first-name plus last-name configuration. What made me even more confused was the fact that, if sung slowly and with a twang, "Take Back the Heart" sounded like something you would hear on the so-called Nashville Network, a slow dance for guys and gals in cowboy boots. And yet the sheet music was probably the oldest I had, and I handled them like museum pieces. Another song with the word "Claribel" on it was "Come Back to Erin" *(CD track 5)*, which I'd also seen in an anthology credited as a folk song. So, I thought, Claribel must be one of Ireland's counties. I believed this for at least three years, until I was given an atlas that was good enough to devote an entire page to Ireland. Even then, I thought that it might have been a county that was renamed in more recent times.

Charlotte Alington Barnard was one of many female writers and composers to use a cryptic pseudonym. Jane Austen wrote as "A Lady", novelist Maria Louise Ramé published under the single word "Ouida", composer and pianist Regine Wieniawski, daughter of the famous violinist Henryk Wieniawski, used "Poldowski", composer and arranger Amelia Lehmann (mother of Liza Lehmann) was credited simply as A.L., which I always assumed was evidence of a lazy typesetter, "Dolores" was Woolwich-born composer Ellen Dickson, and "The Chop Waltz" (Chopsticks) was written by Euphemia Allan, but credited to an invented gentleman called Arthur de Lulli.

The *Grove Dictionary of Music and Musicians* is the most well-

Like novelists Jane Austen and Maria Louise Ramé, Charlotte Alington Barnard worked under a cryptic pseudonym: Claribel (image by kind permission of the Louth Museum, Lincolnshire)

respected reference work on western music: it is the Encyclopedia Britannica, the Bible. It failed me when I was looking for popular song composer May H Brahe, of course, but only eccentrics like me would find that odd. And Claribel *is* there in the *Grove*. Charlotte Alington Barnard is summed up in the 3rd edition, 1927 thus: "Between 1858 and 1869 published some hundred ballads, most of which attained an extraordinary popularity of a transient kind." The next entry is for the Reverend John Barnard, a "minor canon of St Paul's Cathedral" who compiled a collection of cathedral music in 1641. He gets six times the space. The *New Grove* in 1980 finally admits that Claribel published songs from 1854, and that she was "the foremost composer of popular ballads in her lifetime". Considering that the ballad was a dominant form in the nineteenth century, and that just about everyone was at it, this is a major achievement. Interestingly, the contributor indulges in whimsical anachronism to call "Take Back the Heart" a torch song.

By the 2nd edition, Barnard is even given a bit of biographical background, although this contributor sees fit to point out that, having allowed her father to force her to break an engagement, it is "ironic" that she was known for "jilt songs" such as "Won't You Tell Me Why?" Not the sort of observation a critic would make of, say, Ravel or Mendelssohn. But at least this entry from 2001 finally gives her the same amount of space as a minor canon of St Paul's Cathedral.

Claribel wrote not just music, but poetry. Lots of it. And essays, which discussed the importance of being cheerful to one's friends, the danger of giving in to daydreams, how lovely blue is, both as a colour and a word, and recommendations for the arrangement of drawing room plants. "I do not think a prettier group can be made than a circle of white cyclamen, with a pink hyacinth in the centre of a round basket well covered with moss." She also compared the ladylike arts of music and sketching: "Music is a stimulant. Drawing is a sedative. Music craves for a response. Drawing is self-sufficient."

She grew up in Louth, Lincolnshire, where her father, Henry Pye, a lawyer and landowner, oversaw the reclaiming of 300 acres of North Somercotes marshes as agricultural land. At the age of nine, she wrote a 20-verse poem to commemorate the distribution of clothes to the poor. She moved to London after her (paternally approved) marriage to the Reverend Charles Cary Barnard and soon became known in London society for her charming songs, which she would sing, accompanying herself at the piano. She made many friends in London; other women who sang or wrote verses.

Her first published song was to Tennyson's "The Brook" and, wishing to remain anonymous, she used her initials – CAB – to create Claribel, referring back to one of Tennyson's early poems: "Where Claribel low-lieth, the breezes pause and die ... "

The eminent singer Charlotte Sainton Dolby, for whom Mendelssohn had written the contralto solos in *Elijah*, and who had written a few oratorios herself, came across these first published compositions of "Claribel" and recognised their appeal. This was where things started to get exciting.

If reading contemporary references to the songs of May H Brahe is to fall into a vat of warm tea and crumpets, to search out what the papers said about Claribel is like hacking open a hornets' nest. It is easy to think of the Victorians as a fairly polite bunch, men treating women (at least, those of Claribel's class) as delicate little flowers, denying them equal rights, certainly, and perhaps being infuriatingly patronising, but at least courteous.

Not Mr Wood, editor of *The Orchestra,* a music journal of the time. Not Charles Purdy, writer and composer. Not Tom Hood, editor of *Fun*. Not the gentlemen of *The Athenaeum*. Not the writers of the *Saturday Review* or *Punch*. From that first song, "The Brook", Claribel's work became the subject of a satirical cartoon: a lady at the piano sings the lyric "Men may come and men may go, but I go on forever" and a man, listening, ripostes "If that's the case, I shall be one of the men that go!"

It's at least slightly funny, if ungallant. But the amount of nastiness hurled at Claribel for her success is stunning. Many factors seemed to be at play, including professional rivalries with her publisher and promoter, Boosey's. And the biggest bugbear for them all seemed to be the royalty system.

According to William Boosey in 1931, Ballad Concerts in the 1860s "were the outcome of a chat between Madame Sainton Dolby and John Boosey"[3]. In these concerts, singers had the right to earn a percentage of the sheet music sales of the songs they included. And, naturally, a song that was difficult to play or challenging to the ear would sell fewer copies. A song that could be replicated easily by most musicians at home, and appealed upon first hearing would sell very well indeed. Equally, a song presented by an engaging, magnetic personality with a beautiful voice would make even more money for the publishers.

Madame Sainton Dolby became good friends with Mrs Barnard. The two Charlottes discussed music, appeared at the same parties and Sainton Dolby inducted the newly-wedded young composer and poet into higher musical circles as well as giving her singing lessons in her Marylebone home. Soon, Sainton Dolby was pushing the songs of Claribel, spectacularly.

"The great English contralto possesses so many admirers that it is impossible to receive them at one entertainment," gushed one review. She sang "Janet's Choice", and that proved such a success that Boosey's demanded Claribel follow it with "Janet's Bridal", which another popular singer, the tremendously named Euphrosyne Parepa, made popular. Miss Emily Spiller, Miss Poole, Miss Louisa Pyne: many, many singers came forward, wanting to sing anything Claribel wrote and reap the financial rewards. Her songs were performed at lecture halls, penny readings, spas, town halls, the Beethoven Rooms in Harley Street, concert halls and rooms all over the country. The arrangement suited Boosey's, who put Barnard on an exclusive retainer of £300 a year, a very unusual move. It suited the public, who could hear songs they had a chance to replicate at home. It suited the singers, who could earn more in a precarious profession. And it suited the composer herself, whose songs would not have been so well known and widely distributed otherwise.

But it didn't suit the critics.

In 1861, the *Musical Times* recommended, rather nonsensically, that "Claribel hath a tuneful vein; but she must compose less music, and write more poetry". A couple of years later the same publication sneered that "Maggie's Secret", an enormously popular ballad performed by Sainton Dolby at the Crystal Palace, was "a meaningless song" which "broke the spell" of an otherwise good concert. *The Athenaeum* pointedly lamented the advent of "a class of vocal music whose increase tends toward the detriment of public taste" and was still at it in '68 when an article commented that it was a good thing "to have a ballad concert without Claribel-ware – trashy words set to trashy music". The term "Claribel-ware" came from an article the previous year from her most vitriolic attacker, Charles H Purdy.

The eminent English contralto and composer Charlotte Sainton Dolby, who recognised the appeal of Claribel's songs and inducted her into higher musical circles.

Raging against what he perceived as a musical corrosion caused by materialism in art, he predicted in an article in *The Orchestra* – republished elsewhere, including America – that future historians will ascribe the decline of "song music" to the influence of the royalty system, a remunerative speculation pandering to "the illiterate million". He named Claribel specifically and repeatedly, making fun of her verses and music alike, and attacking Sainton Dolby for giving "ignoble aid", her ballad concerts put on for "the purpose of foisting more musical bric-a-brac on the public" and resulting in injury done to the cause of music. "A future state, in which Claribel's old songs constitute the music of the spheres, must be, not to put too fine a point on it, Hades … Claribel-ware eternally". In another article in the same journal, Purdy said "the habit of giving singers a pecuniary interest in the music they sing is making it easier to cram some inane ballad into the ears of all and sundry and is keeping the popular taste low. I have in mind a certain lady who since the royalty system, gets ridiculous tunes sent by a non-musical lady from the country". He followed this with a mocking parody of one of Claribel's most famous works, "I Cannot Sing the Old Songs", ending "I much prefer some rubbish written by Dowzibel/For everyone can sing them/And oh my! Don't they sell".

As it happened, *The Orchestra* was owned by the music seller, publisher and instrument-maker Cramer & Co, with offices on Regent Street, and edited by George Wood, a partner. He didn't like Boosey's at all: he had just lost a court case to them. As to Charles Purdy, John Boosey gave instructions that he was not to be served with any music published by his house. Purdy responded with a laboriously mocking poem called "The Publisher's Revenge", in which he said "What will Claribel say?/Or the Dolby, I pray?/This loss to their profits will floor 'em", etc, etc.

The publicity only served to make Claribel's songs sell more vigorously. She even broke America. After the Civil War, and during Euphrosyne Parepa's 1867 tour, came Claribel-mania. Her gentle songs were exactly what a war-torn, exhausted country needed. More than seventeen different American publishers printed "Take Back the Heart". *The Philadelphia Enquirer* said of Claribel's "Five O'Clock in the Morning", "all the fresh breeze of that early hour, in a warm spring day, among the fields, lanes, beautiful green pastures, are round you while she sings the song, and the charm it wraps round you makes you think of youth, home, holidays … all that is pleasant". "Who would ever tire of listening to angels?" asked the *St Louis Democrat*. Even half a century later, the "White House Music Book" contained no fewer than nine songs by Claribel.

Margate tarted up Spiers and Pond's Hall by the sea when Parepa returned to England. The orchestra was erected in the middle and arched compartments placed all around, lined with white fabric with pink and gold trim. Every third one had a large mirror embedded in a fresh bank of moss with silk flowers impregnated by scents from perfumer Eugene Rimmel – a name still to be seen on cosmetic counters today. All especially for nightly ballad concerts of Claribel's songs.

When Charlotte Barnard wasn't getting ill from the stress of critics' attacks, she was writing music and poems for friends: "Spring Songs" to build a local church, "The Two Nests" for a friend about to be married, "The Bell's Whisper" to raise money for a church clock and a peal of bells, and memorial verses for bereaved friends and acquaintances, including one for Queen Victoria, recently widowed. She was singing and assisting at benefits for all manner of causes, including Louth Working Men's Institute, and answering begging letters from fans. She wrote about her dog; she wrote about willow trees; she found musical inspiration in the fleeting lights and shadows while rowing a boat on a lake in Croxton.

Teenaged girls put notices in *Beeton's Young Englishwoman* listing sheet music they would trade in exchange for specific Claribel songs, amidst questions regarding the propriety of a lady turning the music for a man as he plays the piano, and whether a square or puffed bonnet crown will be worn next season. Another vicious attack came in January 1868, in a magazine called *Fun,* where the editor Tom Hood asserted that Claribel owed her popularity entirely to singers forcing her songs on the public. This time, an exasperated John Boosey took to print in *The Musical World,* saying "many other writers have enjoyed the same chances of popularity as Claribel but with a very different result".

Almost exactly a year after those words were published, Charlotte Alington Barnard was dead. In the summer of 1868, her father Henry Pye was exposed as an embezzler. He'd not only taken county funds, but had ruined several friends, servants and even his daughter and son-in-law. Charlotte and her husband lost £30,000, at a time when £30 would get you a governess for a year. Mr Pye and his wife skipped the creditors by very suddenly moving to Belgium. Charlotte and her husband joined them, and suddenly her income as a composer became very useful indeed. She lamented that she'd not studied music more ambitiously, and went to the

Brussels Conservatoire for further lessons, writing a French song under the name of C Ligny. At around the same time, she wrote a despairing poem, beginning "Listen what the sea sings – 'Never, never more'!/This, the song the sea sings, to the golden shore"[4]. The Reverend and Mrs Barnard secretly went to Dover for a holiday in January 1869, and she died there of typhoid fever, not yet forty.

"The possession of an ear is a great delight; but at the same time I believe it to be rather an enemy than otherwise to music as an art or science," she had written a few years earlier. "If you have an ear, you prefer amusing yourself with it in your own way. You prefer playing things as you please, and how fatal is this to anything like perfection, professionally speaking!"[5]

In this, at least, she does share something with Beethoven: he preferred amusing himself in his own way as well.

Claribel was born and grew up near the sea, died next to it and, in between, lived amidst heaving waves of passionate, conflicting public opinions. Her friend Charlotte Sainton Dolby chose one of her sea poems to set to music after her death *(CD track 6)*. When I sing it, I like to think of the two Charlottes sitting together in 5 Upper Wimpole Street – now a luxury physio clinic – confiding in each other, about music, pain, love and secrets.

Folk Music Suffrage

"Ernest Newman once said to me that if he had the time, he believed he could single out from our wealth of Hebridean melodies those that must have been the creation of one great genius, one great man; and I for sheer contrariness replied, 'why not one great woman?'"

Marjory Kennedy-Fraser, *Pathways of Song*, 1929

THE WONDERFUL BLUE and black speckled Oxford University Press hardcover *Pathways of Song*, picked up at a garage sale on Gower Point, was one of my favourite diva autobiographies.

I swallowed these whole, gorged on them in my teens like a boa-constrictor. *A Singer's Pilgrimage, Men, Women and Tenors, Such Sweet Compulsion, Mary Garden's Story, Melodies and Memories.* Other times, I chewed and licked at them, hiding their bumped and faded covers behind my binders and textbooks at school. Any first-hand accounts of life as a singer in the mid- to late-1800s would do. Far away from the fluorescent lights flickering against the greyness of elementary algebra and textbooks on government-approved clear-cut logging systems, these were full of crown princes, vast trailing, billowing gowns by Worth, pre-war jewelled parures and veiled countesses with pet snakes, playing baccarat in crushed-velvet-hung casinos. Great literature they were not, but I forgave these retired prima donnas their extravagantly bad writing and didn't care if they exaggerated the truth. They were women who reigned supreme in their world.

Marjory Kennedy-Fraser's autobiography was different. For one thing, she'd never been a proper prima donna – no decadence or gem-studded palanquins for her. *Pathways of Song* qualified for the category because she toured and sang, studied Bel Canto in Italy and took me into the studio of Mathilde Marchesi, the most famous teacher of Belle Epoque divas. There's drama: in Nice she loses three of her talented siblings in a fire in the Theatre des Italiens. Then, halfway into the book, we're off to the remote Hebridean Islands.

Pathways of Song was a gust of fresh salt air bursting through all the heady opera house casinos. All the other diva autobiographies made me long to go to Europe, but Marjory's was the only one that allowed me to be content to exist, while I had to, in a small North American coastal town. Kennedy-Fraser is now a legendary figure. She almost single-handedly saved well over a hundred Hebridean folk songs for posterity. Just as these tiny, precarious communities were forgetting the songs that had kept them company through centuries of isolation, Marjory came along to write them down. The horn and apparatus of a gramophone recorder strapped to her back, braving rough crossings in frail ships, going up cliffs and over bog and tussock with her daughter Patuffa, she persuaded elderly women in cottages thick with peat-smoke to sing plaints they'd learned from fairy-mounds, and notated ancient cloth-weaving ballads from crews of girls as they cured herring.

Growing up, I felt she was as exceptional as the Hebridean Islands themselves: small, cut off, quirky. Music teachers, musicians, elderly neighbours, anyone I spoke to, referred to the great Cecil Sharp when it came to folk music. He collected the songs, produced the arrangements and was published again and again along with the great Ralph Vaughan Williams. Cecil Sharp's folk song anthologies found their way into schools, and his name was on the Sunshine Coast Music Festival concert programmes next to the same songs I sang on the beach at dusk with local cats for company: "Oh No John", "Waly Waly", "Searching for Lambs". He also revived the Morris Dance, which I read about and wished I could see for myself.

At the same time, I started to notice that many of the songs I thought were folk songs were composed by women. Claribel was an example, with not only "Come Back to Erin", but also many others. Looking closely at the Scottish song "My Ain Folk" revealed the composer to be the Canadian Laura Lemon. I had three copies of a lovely song called "Juanita" – one credited it as a folk song, one featured the name of a male arranger, and one bore the name of Caroline Norton. I didn't have the internet, or anyone to tell me, but I started to suspect Caroline was the composer. A footnote Kennedy-Fraser gave in chapter 20 of *Pathways of Song* was another eye-opener: Annie MacLeod, later Lady Wilson, while notating a

Songs of the Hebrides

Folk Songs from the Scottish Isles
Collected, Arranged and Sung by

Marjory Kennedy-Fraser
AND HER DAUGHTER
Patuffa Kennedy-Fraser

Available for engagements during season 1916-17 under the management of
J. B. POND LYCEUM BUREAU   Metropolitan Life Building, New York

Marjory Kennedy-Fraser braved rough sea crossings in frail ships to save more than a hundred Hebridean folk songs with the help of her daughter, Patuffa (image by kind permission of Edinburgh University Library)

shanty sung by the fishermen she'd seen hauling up a sail in the summer of 1883, added an extra section of her own invention. This was none other than the famous "Skye Boat Song", and Annie's extra section is the refrain, the bit everyone knows and loves.

Most children are obsessed with getting credit where it is due. I was furious on behalf of these women and longed to pull aside the cloak of anonymity; the world of folk song seemed to be covered in the biggest cloak of all. I wondered how many songs and poems marked "Anonymous" or "Folk" were women. I also wondered if Marjory Kennedy-Fraser was the only female song-collector out there.

In the library, I ran across a transcript of a lecture given in the small hall at Westminster Town Hall at the International Congress of Women in 1899. It was by a Miss Kate Lee and called "Some Experiences of a Woman as Folk Song Collector". Song collecting, she told her listeners in Westminster, was a "healthful pursuit; takes the collector more into the country than the town – stimulates by the charm of unexpectedness" and all one needed was a pencil, a piece of paper and a fine stock of patience. Collecting folk songs added "charming diversion and variety to a dull stay by the seaside or in the country", then you'd "return home triumphantly with a jolly old ballad and produce it to your somewhat incredulous relatives".

She sounded like something out of a novel by Angela Brazil. The Jolliest Madcap Song-Collecting Chum.

I asked everyone about Kate Lee for years. Nobody had ever heard of her. Eventually, I found out that she was a key figure in folk song conservation, one of the people who formed the Folk-Song Society in 1898. The first song published in the society journal was collected by Lucy Broadwood, and the bulk of the rest by Kate, who was also the honorary secretary. It struck me then that her talk at the congress may have been deliberately lighthearted and non-threatening, a jolly hockey sticks attitude to encourage more people to get out there and preserve traditions that were fading fast.

I finally got a chance to read the journals of the old Folk-Song Society in the library in London's Cecil Sharp House. Anyone can go there, and for those who can't, its online resources are amazing. It was there that a librarian told me that Cecil Sharp only collected his first folk song in 1903. Kate had started collecting in 1896.

Despite his late start, Sharp was quickly famous, regarded as an expert almost instantaneously. He'd been invited to join Kate Lee and Lucy Broadwood at the Folk-Song Society in 1901. They were inclusive: Kate invited the great Edward Elgar to come and give a paper on the folk songs he'd collected in Worcestershire in 1899, and in one of the copies I looked at there was an article on Folk Song Survivals in Jewish Worship Music. The society put announcements in journals to encourage people to come forward with songs, one such notice in *Lloyd's Weekly News* bringing an old lady from East London to Kate Lee's flat, the former remarking that she "hadn't ever visited a real lady before". The grand old men of the musical establishment, eminences such as Ivor Boulton and Sir Charles Villiers Stanford, wanted to arrange, rework and polish folk song, make it into art, but Kate Lee, Lucy Broadwood and fellow society founder John Fuller Maitland believed it should be represented exactly as it came from the mouths of the people, in a simple melodic form.

Kate Lee, born Spooner – related to the unintentionally hilarious Professor William Spooner of Spoonerism fame – was a professional singer, trained at the Royal College of Music under William Herschel, Albert Visetti (he was still there in the 1920s to give May Brahe her guided tour) and Frederick Bridge. She sang Wagner, Brahms and Schubert, as well as English, Manx and Irish folk songs. She joined the Irish Literary Society in 1895, and a year later was charming gardeners, workmen, elderly ladies and milkmaids with her direct and simple manner in order to get them to sing their songs, sometimes even posing as a waitress in a country inn.

But she started to slow down in 1900, and meetings of the Folk-Song Society were cancelled due to her ill health. Cecil Sharp said in a letter to the *Morning Post* on January 25th 1904 that "owing to the illness of the hon secretary … the society is in a moribund condition" and proposed starting a rival society to take over. It was an unfortunate choice of words. Kate was dying from ovarian cancer.

Today, Cecil Sharp House is full of life and energy and projects that often involve fascinating cross-cultural collaborations. Its library is named after Ralph Vaughan Williams, who said in an article in 1948 that Kate and Lucy's original Folk-Song Society's proceedings were of a "dilettante and 'tea-party' order"[1]. It is a very beautiful library, one of the most pleasant I've ever been in, with hand-painted gold detailing on black wooden shelves and built-in cabinets with diamond-shaped glass panes. It would be a very nice setting for a tea-party. I found out many things in the three days I spent in it, but it surprised me most that Cecil Sharp was opposed to women's suffrage. I was finding suffragettes all through the folk conservation movement, and only that morning had learned from Marjory Kennedy-Fraser scholar Per Ahlander that the amanuensis of the misty Hebrides had chaired Women's Freedom League meetings and raised money for Edinburgh's suffrage organisations. The more I read about the Edwardian folk revival, the more I found those connected with it involved in campaigning for the vote.

Even the building bearing Cecil Sharp's name was built by a suffragette. I knew this from another Edwardian autobiography by Cecil's sister Evelyn Sharp, famous for her writing and her politics. One fascinating bit is where she lists the sorts of things that were hurled at speakers whilst giving talks supporting votes for women – hard chestnuts being the worst. Fortunately, shortages during the war resulted in fewer vegetables, but the dead (and live) mice and rats continued unabated. The biggest round of applause she received, however, was not for anything she said, but for catching an unexpected egg in mid-air without breaking it.

She went to jail for smashing windows, but like her friends Emmeline and Frederick Pethick-Lawrence, she objected to Christabel Pankhurst's idea of using arson as a form of protest. They were expelled from the Women's Social and Political Union, and formed a peaceful sister organisation, the United Suffragists. During WWI, they started clubs for women and girls to make life bearable during the absence and increasingly frequent deaths of their men. She describes musical sessions at the clubs, including one with cellist Ivor James, who played ragtime tunes to moderate reactions, then broke into a Bach fugue which held them completely rapt. As zeppelins dropped their bombs, the girls sometimes listened to the gramophone; Carrie Jacobs-Bond's "When You Come To the End of a Perfect Day" was one of the records.

I decided to revisit Evelyn Sharp's book at the British Library

– only a half-hour walk from Cecil Sharp House through Camden Town to Kings Cross – and was amazed to find that money for these clubs was raised by working girls' Morris Dance displays, and that these girls had come from the very streets I'd just walked through to get from one library to the other.

I'd finally seen Morris Dancing some years earlier, after singing a recital for Somerset's Frome Festival one summer. A small group of men in white with bells strapped onto their knees were jumping from one foot to another, while their devoted wives stood by with packed lunches, one of them playing a hurdy-gurdy. I stopped for a pint at the nearby pub, the better to stare. "You like that shit?" said the eighteen-year-old behind the bar. "It's a fascinating slice of history," I said. He turned away, muttering: "Slice of shit." Not long after, I read a lighthearted little piece in the *Guardian* by John Crace with some bullet points on how to become part of the twenty-first century folk revival. The first one: "Be male. There are some mixed teams, but they are thin on the ground … more often than not it's the wives and girlfriends who are expected to keep the white shirts, trousers, hankies, etc pristine" (January 7th 2009). But the Morris revival had very feminist roots.

Suffragette Mary Neal began her career in social work at the West London Mission, where she met Emmeline Pethick. They were part of a groundswell of women who believed that what would help the desperate urban poor, as surely as improved nutrition, was a physical connection to their rural antecedents. "Folk music has its roots deep, deep in the rhythm of earth and heaven and sea … those who spin and weave have no tangled threads, no puckered cloth when the shuttle and the loom go with the rhythm of a song,"[2] Mary wrote in the *Espérance Morris Book* in 1910. Mary and Emmeline broke away from the mission to form the Espérance Club for working girls in the shabby, filthy, crumbling tenements of Somers Town, also starting the Maison Espérance, a dressmaker's shop with fair wages and hours, and introducing singing and dancing for all. Mary decided to ask Cecil Sharp to recommend an expert in the Morris Dance, and learned of William Kimber of Headington Quarry in Berkshire. She had Kimber and his cousin take the train to Kings Cross. They stayed two days and, according to Mary Neal, the Kimbers told her that "these London girls had learnt more in two evenings than they could teach country lads in six months"[3]. Soon the girls were teaching other girls, and then they were touring, and participating in events all over Britain. Hundreds of girls in the largest venues of the land were delighting audiences with the Morris.

Around the turn of the century, women lucky enough to have learned the genteel art of music seemed to be emerging from their parlours to share its goodness with those less fortunate. In that same 1899 Westminster International Congress where Kate Lee took to the podium to encourage ladies to notate jolly old songs, there was a presentation on "Music For the People" given by Miss (Ethel) Robinson, secretary of the People's Concert Society, which aimed to blur the line between the classes by making classical music freely available to all. It was run by its honorary secretaries – all women – from its beginnings in 1878. Meanwhile, the People's Entertainment Society saw the Viscountess of Folkestone conducting an all-women choir and orchestra and, in 1888, Alexandra, Princess of Wales, played the piano as her three daughters sang for patients at the Brompton Hospital for Consumptives, an illness then thought highly contagious. In the early 1850s, Octavia Hill, aged just 13, ran a Ladies' Cooperative Guild in Fitzroy Square with her mother, making toys with the poor children of Bloomsbury. She went on to become a ground-breaking housing reformer and founded the National Trust. Her sister Miranda Hill instigated the founding of the Kyrle Society which sought to bring art to hospitals and made gardens of unused land in places like Southwark and Hackney. The Kyrle Society employed the services of the first woman in Britain to work as a landscape gardener, Fanny Wilkinson. It also had a choir to give free concerts in schools and workhouses.

Meanwhile, Grace Kimmins, another West London Mission sister, had gone from Kings Cross to Bermondsey to form the Guild of Play, teaching urban children ancient songs and games. She went on to form the Guild of Brave Poor Things, which encouraged disabled children to look upon their physical challenges like valiant soldiers, while they were fed, clothed, and taught handicrafts and independence. The *Guild of Play Book of Festival and Dance* was

Hundreds of young working women joined Espérance Clubs to learn to Morris dance (image by kind permission of the English Folk Dance and Song Society)

published by J Curwen and Sons in 1907, who also published Mary Neal's *Espérance Morris Book* three years later. In the back of the latter are advertisements for a number of similar instruction books: *Maypole Exercises* by Miss E Hughes, *Old Devonshire Dances* by Mildred Bult, *Greensleeves and Other Old Dances* by Miss Cowper Coles, *Court Dances and Others* by Nellie Chaplin, an astonishing array of *Old Singing Games* volumes from, respectively, Hampshire, the Isle of Wight, Surrey, Breton and others, and also *Skipping Rope Rhymes* and *Old Christmas Carols*. All collected by Alice E Gillington, who apparently lived in a caravan, the easier to gather these ditties.

Mary Neal's Morris-dancing working girls were finding empowerment in the vigorous, team-building dance displays that they so gleefully shared out amongst an increasing number of young women throughout the country and abroad. They started to add their own style to the dances, which evolved as they spread. This new style, along with their startling success, which even led to a cartoon in *Punch* in 1907, alarmed Cecil Sharp. He saw a tradition being corrupted, and his passion was conservation. Charity and art do not mix, he wrote in *The New Age* weekly review. He contrasted the careful scholarship of his Oxbridge colleagues with this other approach "found on the stage of charity matinees or in the flagrant fashion of the Espérance Guild of Morris Dancers, a guild more anxiously concerned about the pretty colouring of the little girls' frocks, mauves and greens and pinks and blues hideously mixed together, than the preservation of a fine and – let it be said – elaborate tradition"[4]. The girls did meet with some prejudice along with their triumphs, as seen in a description by Marjorie Sidgwick of a Morris Dance class in Oxford taught by "an East London club girl, looking about fourteen, almost a slum girl, probably a gypsy, a brown-eyed goblin with feet trained by London barrel organs, taking a class of forty middle-aged schoolmistresses with expert calm"[5].

In December 1910, Mary had taken another of her protegees from the Somers Town slums, Florence Warren, to America. Despite the efforts of Sharp and his colleagues to stop their tour, Florrie danced at Carnegie Hall and trained 200 girls in Albany New York to dance the Morris for 1911's 4th of July celebrations. But when Mary returned to England she found her position increasingly undermined. The war came, girls went to the factories and Grace Kimmins' little Brave Poor Things welcomed amputees from the trenches; the boys teaching the men how to paint with their feet and use wheelchairs confidently to go about everyday life.

Neal and Sharp settled their differences eventually and, after Sharp died, Neal gave donations to help with fellow suffrage campaigner Evelyn Sharp's project to build Cecil Sharp House. The Morris Dance had by then shifted from urban working-class girls to rural upper-class men. One of these, Bedales and St John's Cambridge alumnus Rolf Gardiner, nevertheless wrote of his frustration at the gender imbalance: "Women flocked to the schools and dominated the society's branches. Men were in a hopeless minority. It was a most unnatural state of affairs."[6] He was no fan of Cecil Sharp, writing that he had conjectured the Morris from "the shambling of the greybeards" and that his English Folk Dance Society had "a highly conscious technique, a thing of words and formulae", when what really was needed was masculine vigour. He visited Mary Neal who, interestingly enough, applauded his fresh sincerity and view of the Morris as "a priest's dance of ritual and discipline"[8]. Gardiner went on to rename women's Morris "Werris" and Morris Dancers Morris *Men*. He didn't reject women altogether; he wrote of "a night-time or female purpose", an "elemental unreason from which wisdom is absorbed as nurture is sucked by a tree-root in the soil"[9].

I was prepared to hate everything this woman-excluder said, but that did get me thinking.

From the very first, I'd always sought the elemental unreason of the stretch of beach where the crab-apples leant down to touch the driftwood and waves slopped at the leaves at high tide. That was where folk songs seemed to work best when I was a girl. Whoever had collected the songs, someone had thought of them in the first place, and I knew they hadn't thought of them in a university. When I ran out of words, I sang the melodies with no words at all, thinking of Kennedy-Fraser's peat-fire cottages or isolated mountain communities in early America, houses with tiny windows that let in as little cold as possible; long, silent nights which seem to press in, demanding song as companion, as warmth. Absorbed as nurture. Places where the subconscious may well have formed those tunes, and strange stories of many verses.

"There were actually many female song collectors," Laura told me at the Vaughan Williams Memorial Library. "Many more than are credited. They were known as 'gateway collectors'. They'd find people in the small communities, gain their trust, then connect the singer with the expert, usually male." Maybe it was night and elemental unreason that gained this trust?

I suspect it was also charm.

In a nice reversal, I always knew that Josephine McGill wrote "Duna" *(CD track 7)*, but I didn't know until recently that she was a song collector.

Josephine spent four months in the Kentucky mountains in 1914, riding muleback along rocky creek beds in pursuit of ballads. She wrote: "If they suspect the stranger of a patronising, critical or otherwise superior attitude, likely as not they will decline to share their melodious stores."[10] Josephine's respect for those she collected from is shown in her anthology of *Folksongs of the Kentucky Mountains*, published by the redoubtable Boosey's. "DEDICATION: To those in the Kentucky Mountains 'who take delight in singing', these arrangements are dedicated by 'The strange woman who

Composer Josephine McGill, who wrote "Duna", spent four months collecting songs in the Kentucky mountains in 1914, riding muleback in pursuit of ballads.

went among them looking for Song-Ballets'." She lists nine specific people by name: seven women and two men, as well as the children of the Hindman Settlement School.

"Duna" was one of a few original compositions by Josephine McGill, and I loved to play it because of the big chords. I also liked the words because, unusually for a printed song, they allowed the singer to adjust the gender however they liked. "Man" could be "maid". The text, I didn't realise then, was by a Canadian poet. What was more, Marjorie Pickthall had visited the very beaches I went to for my private folk singing. Both Josephine and Marjorie died far too early: McGill in 1919 at the age of 42, Pickthall in 1922 at 38. McGill doesn't even have a Wikipedia page and Pickthall's online presence echoes to the phrase "no other Canadian writer has suffered such a plunge in reputation as Marjorie Pickthall"[11]. By 1943, critic Edward Brown had written: "When she was faced with the need to sum up civilization, she summed up nature; for her there was nothing else. And the nature she loved was nature in exquisite little details. Naturism could go no further. Marjorie Pickthall had worked the last and smallest lode."[12] Even her biographer and anthologist criticised her in 1957 for a "tendency … toward emotional interpretations of life, and rapture and intuition are substituted for the discipline of reason"[13].

My examination of women in folk song was turning out to be an exploration of subtle variants of the backhanded compliment.

Douglas Kennedy, director of the English Folk Dance and Song Society from Cecil Sharp's death until 1961, wrote in 1984: "Mary Neal was essentially a 'do-gooder', more concerned with giving enjoyment than with the idea of rescuing a threatened species."[14] Even back in 1936, Sorley MacLean wrote of Marjory Kennedy-Fraser's songs and the so-called Celtic Twilight in general: "They have had their hour in the drawing rooms of Edinburgh and London; they have soothed the ears of old ladies of the Anglo-Saxon bourgeoisie."[15] When I finally gathered the courage to sing folk song somewhere other than a deserted beach, I brought volume one of the *Songs of the Hebrides* to the Courtenay Youth Music Camp on Vancouver Island. The song coach looked unimpressed. I asked her why she wasn't as thrilled as I was, and she shook her head: "Marjorie collected these wild songs, then she put prim and proper words on them so they could be sung by genteel Edwardian girls in parlours." As a shy teenager, I didn't have the confidence to tell her that Marjorie made the songs popular and accessible to all by providing singable, English versions that probably thousands of – yes, Edwardian – girls as well as women and men enjoyed, rather than just a few musicologists. Furthermore, she had recorded the original singers and donated those recordings to Edinburgh University.

When Florence Warren, an orphan from the worst slums of London, went to New York with Mary Neal in December 1910, she didn't

Canadian poet Majorie Pickthall, who provided the words for Josephine McGill's "Duna" (image by kind permission of Victoria University Library, Toronto)

end up using her return ticket. A Yale student, remembering the girl who danced the Morris looking like a milkmaid of old, threw down his golf clubs in the middle of a game and ran as fast as he could to the New York docks. He dashed on board before Florrie's ship set sail for Southampton and asked her to marry him. Their daughter ended up dancing under the father of American ballet, George Balanchine.

Not quite a diva autobiography, but an excellent plot for a musical.

Children, Church, Change

WHEN SWISS WOMEN marched peacefully through the streets of Zurich campaigning for the vote, placards reading "*Den Frauen zuliebe – ein männliches JA*" ("The women beg you, give us a gentlemanly yes") they were mocked and jeered at. My nonagenarian friend Helen frequently relived it for me, telling me about men shouting: "You would be better off at home preparing the food for your children than wasting your time out here." Helen not only managed to campaign for women's votes, but raised four children alone, knitted their clothes, cooked their meals, and worked at a laboratory. She did not need someone to tell her how to organise her time.

Another common taunt that greeted them as they held their quiet demonstrations was "Kinder, Küche, Kirche!"

Children, Kitchen, Church.

I've noticed that, when it comes to the practical applications of music, women are suddenly very much in evidence. Symphonies, operas, string quartets are grand, fanciful, showy, but when a baby can't sleep, a child is learning to play the piano, or when a Sunday school needs to take to heart a message of community-binding morality, a song has an immediate practical use. And it is precisely the practical considerations of community – Kinder, Küche, Kirche – that would compel so many women not only to write songs, but to want to have a vote.

Many women's songs are songs by necessity. "Rock-a-bye Baby" was written by Maine actress Effie Crockett when, as a teenager, she found herself in the street with a crying baby left in its pram while its mother was off on an errand. She picked up the baby and improvised a song to calm it down. It was published under the name of Effie Canning, her grandmother's surname, because she thought her father would disapprove. I remember it as one of the first songs I ever sang, amazed even as a toddler how the bough breaking and the baby falling could sound so soothing. Silent film actress Clara Bow used to think of the tune whenever she needed tears for a scene. Now if you look up Effie Canning, you'll find her on IMDB with more than two hundred film-music credits, all for "Rock-a-bye Baby".

"Happy Birthday" was written by sisters Patty and Mildred Jane Hill in 1893 as "Good Morning to All" for their kindergarten and primary school students. It spread throughout the schools of Kentucky, by 1911 acquiring its Happy Birthday words.

"Chopsticks" *(CD track 8)* is the first thing many children play when confronted with a piano and has been for many decades. This was written by sixteen-year-old Glaswegian Euphemia Amelia Nightingale Allan under the pseudonym of Arthur de Lulli in 1877 as the "Chop Waltz". Her father was a dancing master who had hopes his sons would be composers, so Euphemia's brothers were named Haydn, Handel and Mozart Allan. Mozart became a publisher, printing many tartan-bound Scottish song anthologies. Wisely, he also published his sister's "Chop Waltz".

One of the most romantic practical uses of songwriting (according to legend; my queries to the family have gone unanswered) concerned the song "In the Gloaming" *(CD track 9)*. Annie Fortescue Harrison, born in Calcutta the daughter of an MP, came to Hillsborough Castle in Ireland in 1870 or 71 at the age of nineteen, was immensely popular in the community where she visited the cottage tenants, and made herself useful playing the organ at the church. She also befriended the young lord. They fell in love, but his family disapproved of the match, and so she ran away to England without saying goodbye or leaving word as to where she was going.

At that time, Hampshire poet Meta Orred's poems of longing and loss were very popular; to sit down with one of her books is to enter the world of the helpless inner turmoil of a respectable Victorian woman. *Ave*, for example, is a set of twenty-two poems of anguished abandonment that reminds me of *Winterreise*, only without the winter and without the reise.

Whenever I read and sang the poems of Müller and their settings by Schubert, I always wondered about the women who had been similarly jilted and didn't have the freedom to walk off into the winter's night. Probably, they sat and paced in their bedrooms

MP's daughter Annie Forescue Harrison, who had phenomenal success with her song based on Hampshire writer Meta Orred's poem "In the Gloaming".

wringing their hands, their minds circling in tight, fiery knots.

However, Annie did run away, and she managed to write a song about it. She found in one of Orred's books a poem that reflected her situation, "In the Gloaming", and set it to music. The emotional sincerity of this setting was striking, and it was a phenomenal success. At one of its many public performances, Arthur Hill, the young lord, happened to be in the audience, visiting London. Still aching from the disappearance of his beloved Annie over five years earlier, he was moved by the song's message and asked who wrote it. And today, if you look up Annie Fortescue Harrison on the internet, the internet will ask you "did you mean Lady Arthur Hill?" Lord Arthur's parents must have changed their tune quite decisively. After she was married, Annie, Lady Hill wrote two short operas, *The Ferry Girl* and *The Lost Husband*, to librettos by her mother-in-law. She was happily married to her lord for fifty-four years, until his death in 1931. When she died fourteen years later, her parlour organ was donated to the local church where it is still played today.

Annie's tune of "In the Gloaming" is also used for a hymn called "Blessed Bible! How I love it!" with words by Phoebe Worrell Palmer, who died a couple of years after Annie had left Ireland for England, bereft. Phoebe's daughter, Phoebe Palmer Knapp, wrote the music for Fanny Crosby's hymn text "Blessed Assurance". Blind since she was a baby, Fanny Crosby was a campaigner for the education of blind people. As with many women, she believed her inspiration came directly from God, a way that women lyricists and composers frequently side-stepped the fraught issue of ego. Hymnals are full of women, both composers and poets. Before women had proper rights in the eyes of the law, the church and temperance were important ways to maintain a moral standard. And though the popular modern narrative of Victorian church culture often focuses on oppression and guilt, a church-going community was preferable to a drunken and permissive one and it was practical to want to spread the Christian message. In hymnals, Claribel's real name of Charlotte Alington Barnard appears above her tune "Brocklesbury". Its text is "Jesus, Tender Shepherd, Hear Me" by Mary Lundie Duncan, who wrote this poem and several others for her young children in the autumn and winter of 1839. Mary died the next year at the age of 26. The tune of Crimond, the most well-known setting of "The Lord's My Shepherd", was written by Jessie Seymour Irvine, though when it was first published in 1872 it was credited to one David Grant, who had merely arranged it for the psalter. Then there was organist Elizabeth Stirling, whose setting of Psalm 130 "Out of the Deep" so impressed the Oxford examiners in 1856 that they would have awarded her a Music Baccalaureate, but as the *Dictionary of Composers for the Church in Great Britain and Ireland* puts it, they "had no powers" to award one to a woman.

Much of the music of hymns comes from their lilting, breast-swellingly lyrical poems. Julia Ward Howe wrote the poem "Mine Eyes Have Seen the Glory of the Coming of the Lord" after hearing Civil War troops singing "John Brown's Body" when she and her husband were in Washington surveying sanitary conditions of soldiers in the field. She was an abolitionist, suffragist and social reformer who founded women's clubs, the Women's International Peace Association and Mothers' Peace Day in 1873, now known as Mothers' Day. The words for "America the Beautiful" are by Katharine Lee Bates, and Cecil Frances Alexander (not a man, despite her first name) wrote the hymn texts "Once in Royal David's City", "There is a Green Hill Far Away" and "All Things Bright and Beautiful" in a book called *Hymns for Little Children* in 1848. My copy is from 1896, and already a 69th edition; its phenomenal sales built an Institute for the Deaf and Dumb in Strabane, Ireland, and also helped run a Home for Fallen Women in Derry. Also by Cecil Frances is the translation of St Patrick's Breastplate, "I Bind Unto Myself Today". Another inspired translation from ancient Irish is "Be Thou My Vision" by Eleanor Hull, in 1912, and let's not forget the translation from German of "We Plough the Fields and Scatter" from Jane Montgomery Campbell, who led children's choirs in Paddington and wrote a book on choir training for the Society for Promoting Christian Knowledge. These are just the ones that move me when I'm playing and singing them on a Sunday. This list goes on and on, inspiring, unforgettable words that have given courage to and lifted the spirits of millions.

Modern hymns offer a similarly long list of women. Every week churches all over the world sing Estelle White's setting of the Lord's Prayer, or her contemplative, flowing hymn "Gentle as Silence". Estelle wore Chanel No 5, played saxophone for the Auxiliary Territorial Service in WW2, trained as a physiotherapist, entered a convent in Canada, went back to England to be a schoolteacher, directed choirs, and after retiring as a teacher, studied Hebrew and Greek, earning an MA with distinction at 64. In 1996, choristers in Wroxham, Norfolk, found her "Autumn Days", a jaunty children's hymn that praised jet-planes' mid-air refuelling, too modern for their tastes, prompting an article in the *Independent*, where White said: "All my hymns are very clear, very concrete. I don't believe God is vaguely out there sitting up on a cloud with a beard. I think you find the transcendental in everything, so I tend to write hymns that bring in concrete things."[1]

Another modern hymn-writer concerned herself with the concrete of walls, floors and ceilings: Bernadette Farrell, whose "Longing for Light" contains the verse "Longing for warmth, many are cold; make us your building, sheltering others; walls made of living stone"[2]. She often staged sung protest in her capacity as deputy director for London Citizens. They got Tate Modern to raise the wages for its workers by singing Christmas carols in the Turbine Hall – with her own, very pointed, lyrics.

The role of community singing in civil rights struggles in the American South is well documented. The beauty of song brings attention and, once attention is drawn, the message can find its mark. Or in the case of Harriet Tubman, singing hymns saved lives. Her well-worn hymn book is one of the most precious items housed in the Smithsonian Institution; she used hymns as code on the Underground Railroad, a secret network of escape routes and safe houses for enslaved African-Americans. If she sang the same hymn twice, it meant it was safe to come out of hiding. If she sang "Wade in the Water", it was a signal to get into a stream to break the scent trail. "Steal Away to Jesus" meant to get ready for an imminent escape.

Singing makes a physically weak person strong. One of my childhood friends was old Chuck, an enormous biker with a drooping moustache and a booming voice. My favourite story from his turbulent life concerned a fight in a roadside bar in a rough part of Vancouver's East End. A friend of his had said the wrong thing to the wrong people, knives were out and a brawl was starting. Only, Chuck had a back injury from a recent smash-up and was powerless. "But I had my voice," he said to me. Seated with his crutch, he took a deep breath and shook the rafters with "I fell in love with love". Everyone was floored, confused, a couple of them laughing awkwardly, and the fight stopped in its tracks. My activist friend Valerie speaks fondly of the songs of Greenham Common. There the women sang Naomi Littlebear Morena's "You can't kill the spirit, she's like a mountain" and Peggy Seeger's "Hand in hand the line extends" ("Carry Greenham Home"), encouraging the heart-stirring, strengthening feeling of a presence even larger than the immediate physical one. A community that sings seems bigger and stronger than a community that is silent.

A century and a half earlier, it was a sense of Kinder-Küche-Kirche practicality that brought about a revolution in community singing that transformed entire populations, and gave music literacy to the poor for the first time in history.

When Sarah Glover's sister was trying to teach a young Sunday Schoolmaster how to sing in 1812, Sarah, a Norwich rector's daughter known for her excellent work with church choirs, had an idea. She later wrote: "It occurred to me that if I pasted letters over the keys of the pianoforte, and then expressed the tune in letters corresponding with those placed over the keys in the order

Norwich rector's daughter Sarah Glover revolutionised the teaching of music by using a simple lettering system while working with groups of workhouse children.

in which they were to be touched, the youth might teach himself without occupying my sister's time."[3] Success with the tone-deaf schoolmaster was limited, but children at the workhouse responded astoundingly well, so Sarah and her sister continued to explore the idea and, in Glover's words, "the theory of music, disencumbered by the mystery thrown around it by sharps and flats" was quickly understood. In a few weeks, children were singing in two, four or even eight parts, with accuracy and good intonation. Glover's emphasis on harmonic singing was based on the principle of inclusion, "otherwise good voices, male and female, are necessarily silent, because the upper part is not within their compass"[4]. Despite reports of people in authority saying, mystifyingly, that teaching music scientifically to children at a charity school was "dangerous", the results were astonishing and, after twenty years' evolution of the method, Glover published it in a pamphlet in 1835, anonymously.

It spread slowly, but when the first school inspectors started to write reports on the new government-funded schools in 1839, they recorded and shared their amazement at this unprecedented, stunning development in school singing which, furthermore, did not require expensive music engravers. Any printers could produce readable music in "Norwich Sol-fa". The method was taken on by Congregationalist Minister John Curwen. Curwen adapted it, started the Tonic Sol-Fa Association in 1853, published a course of lessons, a periodical called *Tonic Sol-fa Reporter and Magazine of Vocal Music for the People* and created a Tonic Sol-Fa College. Editions of the major classical choral works of Handel, Haydn, Bach and Mozart were printed using the system, and industrial villages and towns, where people had neither the time nor money for "classic" music education could suddenly start to read complex music in four-part harmony. Communities revived, whole valleys thundered in song, Catholics sang the Lutheran music of Bach, chapel-goers sang Schubert masses, and feuds were forgotten as neighbourhoods were divided instead by soprano, alto, tenor and bass.

As for my friend Helen in Switzerland, she told me that an elderly English suffragette once visited and gave her group in Schaffhausen a green, violet and white banner to display on the day when her Swiss sisters got the vote. It was kept neatly in a drawer and was very fragile and faded when the day finally came in 1971. "We had very quiet protests, we were polite," Helen said.

I wonder what would have happened if they'd sung.

The Power of Cupcakes

Despite her dismissal of Parlour Song, Mrs Stuart was a goddess amongst piano teachers. She gave my struggling parents a cut rate, always let me choose the pieces from the Royal Conservatory Syllabus that I liked best, and knew how to combine sternness and warm encouragement with the precision and inspiration of a master mixologist.

Above all, she knew that working towards the annual music festival and the occasional RCM exam were insufficient for discovering the magic of performance.

So, she hosted student recitals at her home several times a year. Valentine's Day, Easter, summer, Hallowe'en and Christmas, we'd all learn what it was to share music with one another, and have a rare chance to find a way to express emotion to a room of peers. Then, we'd troop into Mrs Stuart's kitchen to feast on cupcakes, iced with pink, white and red hearts for Valentine's Day, pastel coloured eggs and bunnies at Easter, yellow suns and flowers in summer, bones, skeletons and spiders in orange and black for Hallowe'en, and green and red holly and reindeer at Christmas, when our parents were also invited.

These recitals prevented me from quitting piano as a repetitive chore that kept me indoors after coming home from school. The fact that each piece I played had a human destination, a room where it would be shared, gave life to the whole endeavour. The cupcakes were, literally and figuratively, the icing.

We were deeply lucky to have Mrs Stuart as a teacher.

Songs as Gifts

In his preface to Carrie Jacobs-Bond's memoirs, Robert MacAlarney wrote: "Uttering unsophisticated affection for God, nature, sweetheart, child, friend or native land calls for bravery in 1927." Though this was the year May Brahe wrote "Bless This House" and definitively proved her worth to publishers Boosey & Co. Clearly, if you got it right, fortune favoured the brave, even in 1927.

But, concluded MacAlarney: "Sentimentality wears well, if it is true Sentimentality."[1] Quite.

Carrie's great success had come a few years earlier.

As a child, I took great delight in sorting my sheet music collection into categories. Waltz, war, women's names, mothers, moonlight, modes of transport. It gave me the collector's tactile thrill of handling it which, back then, made me think of a cartoon tycoon, sifting his fingers through the gold coins in his sacks.

The categories varied a lot; to change them or refine them was another excuse to get in there and handle all those wonderful old song sheets again.

But Carrie Jacobs-Bond always had a category of her own: like Bartok in the local Sunshine Coast Music Festival, who was considered so "other" that he had his own trophy. Poor Bach, Beethoven, Chopin and Shostakovich had to be thrown, with their contemporaries, into the respective boxes of baroque, classical, romantic and twentieth century.

Carrie Jacobs-Bond's music was bigger than other music. Literally. Wide and tall, it had a pearly finish that prevented it from yellowing or getting tattered at the edges, and it had no crass announcements on the back or advertisements shouting "You Can Play the Banjo in Five Lessons" or commanding you to "Buy the New Talking-Machine". Jacobs-Bond covers all had the same design of a branch of roses, painted in beautiful pinks, greens and russets and a guarantee that the songs were "As unpretentious as a Wild Rose". Three songs in particular found their way to the piano:

Carrie Jacobs-Bond managed to capture each phase of life in iconic, definitive songs (image by kind permission of Iron County Historical Museum, Michigan)

"I Love You Truly", "Just A-Wearyin' For You" and "A Perfect Day".

My piano teacher was dismissive of my collection of paper antiques, the internet had yet to be generally accessible and I was too young to drive, so the only way I could find out about the world's relationship with these old sheets was by walking the beach and visiting the retirees who lived along it.

I put the music in plastic bags, put the bags in another bag and, holding it tightly against Squamish gales, hopped from log to log and climbed the slippery cliffs.

Mrs Eckford lived perched over one such cliff, her reddish-brown wooden house surrounded by fir trees and the biggest rhododendrons I'd ever seen.

"'Just A-Wearyin' For You' was how Mr Eckford wooed me," she said. "It's so mournful, I sort of felt sorry for him."

Further along were the Parker Sisters, who lived in two enormous houses above the water with their respective husbands, and despite their having taken the husbands' names, were still very much the Singing Parkers. As girls, they used to entertain the hardened old men of the Yukoners Association, who'd gone prospecting in the early 1900s. When I knew them, they sang for the Tiny Tot Drop-Off.

"Oh yes, 'I Love You Truly'. That was our number one wedding song. I sang that one more times than all other wedding songs combined," said Jean. Pops, very much the Bob Hope to Jean's Bing Crosby, chimed in: "We all had to get married back then Patricia. Otherwise we weren't allowed to have sex."

In the other direction, past the boulders and a sudden smooth stretch of sand, were a series of houses, now long gone, much too close to the tide-line for modern planning permissions. In one of them, a cold shingle house with peeling cream paint and a variety of interesting looking driftwood on its porch, a very elderly lady lived alone. She didn't read music or have a piano but knew "A Perfect Day" so well she could sing the whole thing to me. I'd heard of this song even before finding the music. "When You Come to the End of a Perfect Day" older people would sometimes quote, sarcastically, if things went terribly wrong. Miss Baylor didn't quote it with sarcasm. She meant every word and told me she sang it every time she saw the shadows of the fir trees lengthen over the sea at sunset. "Every day in this house is that kind of a perfect day, and I think of friends who are dead, and feel that happy melancholy tiredness. I don't know who composed the song, but he knew exactly how I feel. I find that quite wonderful."

I was proud to be able to tell Miss Baylor that the person who wrote both the words and the music was a woman. "Well then, no wonder!" she said, waving her hand.

Love, marriage, wistful memory. Carrie Jacobs-Bond managed to capture each phase of life in iconic, definitive songs; songs that symbolised these fundamental aspects of life for three generations. I was in awe. The Parker sisters gave further details. "Carrie Jacobs-Bond was smart. She refused to have anyone else publish her work. She did it all herself. She even designed the covers."

When I was at college and had access to a handful of libraries, I went straight in to look up Carrie Jacobs-Bond. She had started writing music at the age of four and, at eight, played the piano for "Blind Tom" Bethune (not to be confused with "Blind Boone", who was the same age as Carrie, and with whom she later became friends.) She lamented in her autobiography that she heard greater music in her head than she could get down on paper and regretted having been limited to songs. But she grew up in remote north Michigan and only heard her first opera at the age of 20. Though she may have had a certain family affinity with songs: her grandmother's cousin was John Howard Payne, who wrote the words for "Home Sweet Home."

Moderately well-off as a girl, her father lost everything in a "grain panic", and she tried to go to work at a milliners' at the age of 12, to her grandfather's fury: "I guess the men of this family will always be able to take care of our women folks." She wed, divorced, and then was happily married to a doctor, and moved to Iron River. The iron mines closed and not only did the couple lose their investments, but none of the outstanding medical bills could be paid by the destitute populace. She went to the *Chicago Herald* to see if they would print her songs, and Mrs Holden, a reporter with the pen-name "Amber", invited her to come to the Bohemian Club that evening. With a beer keg in one corner and a coffee urn in another, a long table and a piano, Carrie played and sang to a cheerful company of poets, newspaperwomen and men. A publisher asked her if she could write a children's song, and she responded in a couple of days with "Is My Dolly Dead?"; "I dropped dolly – broke her head/Someone told me my doll's dead". It was inserted into a revue called *Fourteen Ninety Two* and had a great success. Shortly thereafter, her husband, Dr Bond, was pushed by a playful child in the snow outside their house. He took five days to die of his injuries.

Jacobs-Bond's memoirs are full of personal anecdotes and stories of individuals who helped her. After her husband died, she painted designs on porcelain tea sets and plates and her friends bought hand-painted porcelain as gifts for everyone they knew. She gave music recitals at friends' homes for $10 a night, and in this way met other people who liked her playing and her songs. Mrs Henry Howe, president of the 20th Century Club in Marshalltown, Iowa, had her come and perform in all the major Iowa towns. In Bloomfield, she saw a lecture by Elbert Hubbard, who with his wife Bertha had founded the Roycrofters, a hugely influential American Arts and Crafts movement, with printing presses in buildings that looked like churches, which were used to spread progressive views in gorgeous woodcuts.

She played her songs for the Roycrofters and was inspired by their printing-press know-how to publish her own music. She got the money together by ringing up Chicago prima donna Jessie Bartlett Davis from a drugstore round the corner – telephones still rarities in 1901 – and visiting the friendly diva at her home. Davis had the 39-year-old widow sit down at the Steinway in her music room and play the songs she'd been talking about. So, Carrie Jacobs-Bond, already suffering from "inflammatory rheumatism" and unable to do anything else but write and perform songs, played the seven she had with her, which included two of her three greatest-ever hits, "I Love You Truly" and "Just a-Wearyin' For You". Jessie Bartlett Davis served tea and then wrote out a cheque, telling Bond to print the music as soon as possible because she wanted to perform them right away. Once printed, Carrie found a woman who owned a music magazine and offered to sew in exchange for advertising.

Her songs sold phenomenally well, but her big hit came nine years later in 1910, when she was in Riverside, Connecticut and saw Mount Rubidoux at sunset. She scribbled down the words for "When You Come to the End of a Perfect Day" *(CD track 10)*, and then a few months later, when she gazed at the moonlight on the Mojave Desert, the tune came to her, fully formed. That song sold in the tens of millions. It was arranged for high, medium and low voice, voice with cello obbligato in two different keys, duet for soprano and alto, duet for baritone and alto, quartets for men's, women's or mixed voices, piano solo, violin, cello and piano, two violins and piano, cornet and piano, C saxophone and piano, E flat sax and piano, piano duet, cello and piano, violin and piano, organ, military band, concert band, concertina and even a waltz version for those who insisted on dancing to it. And the hotel where she first thought of the words, overlooking Mount Rubidoux, had the bells in its belfry play it every evening at sunset.

Even Jacobs-Bond herself grew tired of hearing the song after a while, until, at a barracks, her voice was joined by ten thousand young men bound for Europe. It became a great favourite in WW1 in the same way May Brahe's "Bless This House" was to catch on in WW2. Soldiers sang it in the trenches, sometimes as gallows-humour, or sometimes in a heartfelt desire to think of home. Then, on the day of the Armistice, the crowds in New York all joined together with their hands on each others' shoulders all the way down Fifth Avenue from the Plaza Hotel on 59th to Washington Square Park, fifty-three blocks, all singing "When You Come to the End of a Perfect Day".

The same year she wrote her most famous song, she also published a lovely little book called *Half Minute Songs, (CD track 11-22)* prettily tied up with a ribbon, musical equivalents of the Roycroft Mottos. The mottos were beautifully illuminated sayings, often framed in a nod to the cross-stitch sampler. Roycrofters printed aphorisms like "Fences are only for those who cannot fly", "Imagination is sympathy illumined by love and ballasted by brains" or "Never explain; your friends do not need it and your enemies will not believe you anyway". One still finds them on Pinterest and Instagram (#roycroftpress); an interesting mixture of inspiration, idealism and slightly crusty whimsy in a font as distinctive as anything Charles Rennie Mackintosh created. Similarly, Bond's themes are striving and friendship. And perhaps a little message for us, when she chose to put the statement "Success never comes to the sleeping" to the tune of the first phrase of "A Perfect Day". The melody and words to her number one hit possibly hadn't come as quickly or fully formed as legend had it. And "I'd rather say 'you're welcome' once, than 'thank you' a thousand times" could be the result of having to rely on so many good turns to get her started.

Or it could also be an encouragement to others to keep those good turns coming, encouraging people like herself.

Reading this sort of story was heady stuff to a student. The religion of the Roycrofters' artistic can-do, painting china for money until a diva gives you a cheque for your seven lovely songs. She even travelled for free on the Santa Fe railroad in exchange for giving concerts at the Santa Fe railroad reading rooms. That, basically, was perfection as I imagined it. I wanted all of that and more. I had no idea how I would get it, but Carrie Jacobs-Bond gave me the feeling that there are many odd, untried paths to be taken, and that I didn't have to fixate on one particular goal and feel like a failure if I didn't get it.

Looking back on the days of wandering the beach with old music carefully held between my body and my mum's old purple coat while being splashed by the salty waves, it seems like someone else's past, decades earlier than it actually was. These ladies visited each other, played each other's pianos, made soup for the unwell and read aloud to the very frail. Jean and Pauline liked to read out Patience Strong, who wrote hundreds of poems for funerals, weddings and mothers; anthologised and published in *Woman's Own* or *Good Housekeeping*. I didn't know then that she also wrote song lyrics under her real name, Winifred May, and was responsible for "Jealousy, 'twas only through Jealousy". My parents mocked the poems as doggerel, but when I saw Jean reading one to her hundred-year-old mother I knew they weren't meant to be pored over and analysed, they were meant to be absorbed easily upon first hearing, mellifluous and direct, while breastfeeding, between stirring the stew, turning down the heat on the potatoes, hanging up the washing or for a precious few moments while a centenarian opens her eyes before drifting off again. "Go into the woodland/If you seek peace of mind."

I sometimes played the piano pieces I was going to compete with in the music festival for our neighbours. Even the jagged works of Bartok. I was fiercely competitive, and I'm sure I said some caustic things about the other kids in the festival. "Remember, friendship is more important than winning competitions," Jean said to me. "Visiting and playing is the most precious gift."

A quarter century later, I visited Jean in a hospice. She had dementia. I found her trembling and crying that she was in this strange place, and not greeting me in her home. "Patricia, they tell me I *live* here!"

I'd forgotten to bring chocolates or grapes. And I didn't have any Patience Strong with me. But there was a piano in the hospice, so I played and sang Carrie Jacobs-Bond, and her straightforward message of the importance of the gift of friendship. Instantly, Jean relaxed and smiled, home again.

Sisters of the Organ Bench

Andrea Kmecova and I met during the recording of my second CD, *Our Lovely Day*. She was hired by Matt and Nick, the arrangers of the album, and I didn't know her name until we met at the first of the ensemble rehearsals. To my amazement, this pianist turned out to be the other organist at St Mellitus, the gal who sat on the organ bench when I wasn't on it. I'd never met her – she played when I wasn't available, and I played when she wasn't.

The album was recorded over three days and Andrea's bits weren't scheduled until the second half of the last day. She came into my booth with a tiny tealight candle and set it down. "A little something for calm," she said. She, and the flickering flame, changed the atmosphere of the entire place: settled it, expanded it and made it cosy at the same time. Our tracks were the better for it. Not long after, we made an appearance together at a church fundraiser, astonishing the congregation as their two organists transformed – like two cocooned caterpillars spreading colourful wings – into pianist and singer. It was then that she agreed to join me on this project. We are friends as well as colleagues and we never seem to know if a visit will be social or musical. It is lovely to have a relationship where the two are interchangeable.

Two Identities in South London

"It was with something like awe that we entered the rooms to find no other representative of the sterner sex present..." So wrote the critic for *The Era* on June 23rd 1888, continuing: "Ladies to left of us, ladies in front of us, ladies to right of us, beaming and whispering, and, we fear, indulging in a little jocularity at the solitary masculine visitor." It was a recital featuring Amanda Aldridge and her sister Luranah at Messrs Collard and Collard's Rooms in Grosvenor Square. They sang "The Venetian Boat Song", "A Summer Night", "The Garden of Sleep", and Luranah later sang "The Nubian Girl's Song". Interestingly, the reviewer doesn't mention that Luranah and Amanda, to the average Englishman like him, and spectacularly unusually for Collard and Collard's Rooms, *looked* like Nubian girls.

This chapter is about a surprising, eventful corner of history, seen through the lives and songs of two south Londoners: Amanda Aldridge and Avril Coleridge-Taylor. Both were born into a Victorian world (Amanda in 1866, Avril in 1903, only two years after the Queen's death), they both received music scholarships and they were both of African descent. Their fathers were, each in his own way, trailblazing pioneers and civil rights campaigners. Amanda's father, Ira, was from New York and descended from slaves, and Avril's father, Samuel, was born in Croydon, the son of a doctor from Sierra Leone. Both fathers had attained spectacular success in their respective fields – acting and composing – and their daughters went on to appear in some of the finest concert halls in the land. Avril was the first woman to conduct the band of Her Majesty's Royal Marines and also directed the BBC Symphony, the LSO and the South African Broadcasting Corporation Symphony Orchestra. She wrote a ceremonial march in 1957 for Ghana's independence. Thirty-seven years Avril's senior, Amanda Aldridge's *Three African Dances* and *Four Moorish Pictures* were recorded, broadcast and used in films. She also taught singing and diction to some of the most important African-American singers and actors of the

Amanda Aldridge's ragtime-flavoured compositions were influenced by her African-American heritage.

twentieth century, including Paul Robeson and Marian Anderson, and Nigerian nationalist Herbert Macaulay.

It is a tale of triumph in unlikely times, of which not only south London, but Britain should be very proud. But despite the glory, the prosperity and the apparent middle-class gentility in some of Croydon's most respectable, leafy streets, tragedy loomed over both families like a curse.

Samuel Coleridge-Taylor, who preferred his friends to call him Coleridge because Samuel sounded like the childhood taunt of "Sambo" (they adapted to "Coaley" with the ingenuity of many bullies), wrote operas, symphonies, chamber music, songs and, most successfully, the *Song of Hiawatha,* a secular cantata that had an astonishing success on both sides of the Atlantic. He was hailed as a hero in America and a Samuel Coleridge-Taylor society comprising 200 African-American singers was formed in Washington DC in 1901. He was friends with Paul Laurence Dunbar, the African-American poet, and the two collaborated on an opera, a one-acter called *Dream Lovers*. Confronted with the endless sea of white faces at the Royal College of Music, he developed a theory that Beethoven must also have had some African heritage. Unsure of his own worth, he sold *Hiawatha*'s manuscript for a far smaller amount than he should have and watched, helpless, as it took off and the publishers raked in cash that could have been his. He travelled to as many places as he could, adjudicating students, conducting and rehearsing an endless stream of amateur choirs and orchestras, presenting his works to audiences throughout the British Isles, as well as Boston, New York, Detroit, Toronto, Pittsburgh and Washington DC, holding down teaching positions at Trinity College of Music, the Guildhall School, Croydon Conservatoire and the Crystal Palace School of Music, and working through pneumonia when he should have been resting. In 1912, he collapsed on the platform of West Croydon station, staggered home and died a few days later while checking the parts for his violin concerto from his bed. He was thirty-seven, and left an unfinished opera and many other works that were not to be. Avril was nine. A strange two-dimensional statue of Samuel Coleridge-Taylor stands like a rusting ghost between Ronnie Corbett and Dame Peggy Ashcroft on Croydon's Charles Street between a brutalist high-rise and a car park.

The actor Ira Aldridge had found success a number of decades earlier. His likeness, as Othello, can be seen in a select few museums; Pietro Calvi created ten versions of him in the early 1870s, black marble for his face and hand, contrasting with the cream-coloured marble of his cloak and Desdemona's handkerchief. From poverty-stricken beginnings in New York's Lower Manhattan, Ira Aldridge fell in love with the works of Shakespeare and became a master tragedian, by all accounts not in the forced, artificial style so common in those days, but realistic to the extent that women fainted and men sprang up onto the stage to try to intervene in some of the more dramatic moments. He moved to Europe, inventing a Royal Sudanese origin-story, and married a Swedish opera singer who similarly billed herself as a baroness. Together they had two girls and a boy. He also cared for a son from a liaison some years prior. When Amanda, the youngest, was barely seventeen months old, he died while on tour in the Polish city of Lodz. The whole place turned out to mourn him, giving him a military guard of honour, with the president of the city following the coffin, all the town's guilds carrying their banners and a choir of a hundred singing Haydn.

His eldest, so-called illegitimate boy was by this time in Australia trying to be an actor like his father, but with humiliating results. He then became a schoolteacher but the children made fun of the colour of his skin. He never received his father's intended legacy of £500 and married into a cheque-forging family, which soon forced him into plying their trade. He was in and out of prisons and work-camps until his unrecorded death. According to the records, his children also ended in tragic destitution. Of Ira's three other children, the younger boy was sent to a boarding school in Paris while his parents toured Europe, where he was persecuted and racially abused, becoming sickly and delicate for the rest of his life. He became a talented pianist and composer, commended by the legendary virtuoso Hans von Bülow, gave concerts and accompanied his sisters in recitals. Then, when he was barely twenty, while in Scarborough directing a production of the operetta *Manteaux Noirs,* he was struck down with a lung affliction that made him so desperate for air, he climbed out of a third-storey window and fell to the ground. He died of concussion and his young widow became a lifelong alcoholic.

Luranah, named after her father's New York mother, and the singer so adored by the girls at Collards and Collards' Rooms, seemed set for a brilliant career. She spent some years in Paris, became a friend of Georges Sand, sang one of the Rhine Maidens at London's Royal Opera House and was engaged to perform at the 1896 Bayreuth Festival at the invitation of Wagner's widow Cosima. She stayed at the Wagner home and became friends with Cosima and their daughter Eva, who was later associated with Nazis and whose coffin was draped with the swastika flag. Unfortunately, before her appearance, Luranah lost her voice. Eva and Cosima sent her to an expensive sanatorium to recover, but she'd missed

Amanda and Luranah Aldridge, daughters of the renowned master actor Ira Aldridge, who both had promising but ill-fated singing careers.

crucial rehearsals and the Rhine Maiden had to be sung by another contralto. It wasn't until sixty-five years later, when Grace Bumbry sang Venus in 1961's *Tannhauser*, that Bayreuth was to feature a diva of colour. Luranah returned to England, where she started to suffer from chronic arthritis and depression.

Amidst all this tragedy, the youngest sibling, Amanda, had managed to do very well indeed. In 1883, she was one of the very first group of students to be taken in on a full scholarship by the Royal College of Music. Her father's profession is listed in their records as "Tragedian". She studied with George Herschel and with Jenny Lind, frequently acknowledged as one of the greatest opera singers who ever lived, who was also a friend of her mother's and admirer of her father's. Lind apparently never gave written testimonies, but she made an exception for Amanda Aldridge. Both she and her mother told her to be proud of her African heritage, and she added her father's name "Ira" to her own. It was all systems go for Amanda Ira Aldridge until performing through laryngitis damaged her voice and ended her singing career. She found herself being nurse to a bedridden mother and an invalid sister instead. A Jamaican doctor who had seen her sing at Steinway Hall asked her to marry him, but she turned him down, telling him that what was left of her family was in desperate need of her. Dr Phillips went back to Jamaica, never married, and corresponded with her until his death in 1937.

Her mother had lost everything to an unscrupulous builder and solicitor after Ira's death and the distraught widow melted down all of his decorations, medals and honours for gold to pay off mortgages, including the most prestigious and exclusive honour in the world at that time, the Order of the Knights of Saxony. The sisters and their mother moved to an apartment in Bedford Gardens, Kensington, next door to composer Frank Bridge. With the girls' past friendships and connections, and Amanda's teaching and coaching, many famous people came and went. Their mother died of bronchitis in 1915 and, in 1932, wheelchair-bound Luranah, unable to take her enforced idleness any longer, took an overdose of aspirin. She had a change of heart at the last minute and called out to her sister, in French, to send for a doctor. She died on the way to hospital.

There is enough material in these stories to make three movies at the very least, or better still a TV series spanning the 1860s to the 1950s, to outdo *Downton Abbey* in drama while offering more ethnic variety and better music.

But my own way in to these stories is through my sheet music collection. And both women, Amanda Aldridge and Avril Coleridge-Taylor, are to be found there.

Avril sometimes appears under the name she was born with, Gwendolyn Coleridge-Taylor, and sometimes as Avril. Amanda Aldridge wrote under the moustachioed Victorian moniker of Montague Ring.

And as such, 'his' compositions tend to be culled from stacks of old sheet music because they appear, at first glance, to be a bit racist.

"My Little Corncrake Coon", "Little Missie Cakewalk", "When the Coloured Lady Saunters Down the Street", "Summah is de Lovin' Time"; it all looks an awful lot like the sheet music I stuck in a manila folder and marked "KKK" when I was a girl, then later threw into a bonfire aged 17. I definitely wasn't going to look at or leave lying around antiques entitled "Each Morn' I Brings Her Chicken (That at Daybreak I Have Stole)" with photos of white people in blackface making antic gestures. But on closer inspection, Amanda's songs aren't like those at all.

For example, the text for "Summah is de Lovin' Time" is by Paul Laurence Dunbar, an American cultural treasure. He was the son of freed slaves, worked at the Library of Congress and was the first poet, black or white, to do a poetry reading there. As mentioned previously, he was friends with composer Samuel Coleridge-Taylor. Both he and his daughter Avril set his verses. As to Amanda "Montague Ring" Aldridge's "When The Coloured Lady Saunters Down the Street" *(CD track 23)*, the word "coloured" was the most respectful term in the vocabulary at the time, and yet to be associated so strongly with segregation laws. This was an era when "black" meant "of bad character" (blacklist, blackball, blackguard; the old Irish song "I Know Where I'm Going" with its line "some say he's black/But I say he's bonny"). As to the lady herself, she's an object of desire. She holds her head high and she's described as a "divinity". Amanda herself wrote the words. This song and "Little Missie Cakewalk" are clearly inspired by the sensational success of the African-American Revue *In Dahomey* which came to Britain in 1903. The queens of the Cakewalk were Louisa Gaston in her furs and silks, and star choreographer Aida Overton Walker. It played for several months at the Shaftesbury, then toured Woolwich, Newcastle and Sheffield. Twenty-seven-year-old Samuel Coleridge Taylor went to see it. And, far from being snobbish about this energetic, kaleidoscopic display of folk, pop and ragtime colour, Amanda Aldridge, the eminent daughter of one of the finest-ever Shakespearian tragedians, scholarship student in the Royal College of Music's first-ever year and favourite of Jenny Lind, decided that ragtime ditties, songs about Cakewalk, were just fine.

In these 1910s songs, Amanda always includes an instrumental dance. These really came alive as Andrea played them. I was amazed at how they sprang out of the piano. We sight-read through them on a sunny but cold International Women's Day in Andrea's flat near Greenwich. Then as Andrea was playing "Little Missie Cakewalk", she spontaneously broke into the dazzling octaves of the opening of Grieg's piano concerto. I laughed and applauded in delight. "Same key, sort of same feel," said Andrea. So, as well as embracing African-American idioms, Amanda had found room for a bit of her Scandinavian heritage, melding it into one irresistibly energetic and joyous musical entity.

It was this powerful will to adapt, perhaps, that ensured that Amanda Aldridge evaded the family curse and lived until the eve of her ninetieth birthday.

Avril Coleridge-Taylor was born the same year that *In Dahomey* went on its whirlwind tour of England, and when her eminent father became a fan of its star, Bert Williams. But her songs are far away from ragtime and minstrels. When I put "Can Sorrow Find Me" *(CD track 24)* in front of Andrea, she sighed with pleasure. "Real music," she said as she went through one sophisticated chord after another. The text is by Minnie Aumonier, whose quotes have flowered on the internet and are often used in conjunction with a beautiful photo or two. Someone decided she was an 18th century poet and this has spread, but she was actually born in London in 1866 amongst a family of writers, sculptors and architects. In some sources, she is shown to be a costume designer. She wrote gift books for garden lovers, lived in Finchley, north London, and her books *The Poetry of Gardens* and *Gardens in Sun and Shade* were favourites of the Royal Horticultural Society, where her watercolours were exhibited. Probably her most-shared quote is: "There is always music amongst the trees in the garden, but our hearts must be very quiet to hear it." Another woman of parlour song, Guy d'Hardelot (Helen Rhodes), set one of her poems, "Take All Thy Sorrows", to music. Aumonier's poem "Can Sorrow Find Me?" is darker, and so is what Avril Coleridge-Taylor does with it.

We went through the song, Andrea throwing her arms into the arpeggios, me putting my back into the long high note at "I have grown old in sorrow's chill" and then the pause – surely a moment

Avril Coleridge-Taylor (from the Samuel Coleridge-Taylor family archive by kind permission of Avril's grandchildren Paul Dashwood and Caroline Preece)

when an audience might think it was all over and start to applaud – before the uncertain, disquieting repetition of the first question. After the last bar we stopped and looked at each other. We spoke at the same time: "What on earth happened to Avril? Was she assaulted?"

Her autobiography *The Heritage of Samuel Coleridge-Taylor* explains some things. Reading between the lines of her mother's book *Genius and Musician: Samuel Coleridge-Taylor* supplies a bit more. Her mother, Jessie, was an extraordinary woman to be able to stand up to the constant glares, titters and whisperings she and her African-British husband were treated to. More than stand up to them, she positively rounded on them, giving loudly as good as she got. She was fiercely protective of her husband and quelled the objections of her middle-class family when she announced her engagement, bending them to her will. But this will, like any effective weapon, could harm as well as protect. And it would appear that Jessie resented the love her husband gave their daughter and, according to Avril, even tried secretly to give her up for adoption. From the time she was a little girl of four or five, Avril, then still called Gwendolyn, liked to play at being a composer while her father worked, sitting by him and echoing his actions with pencil and manuscript paper. They walked together through the streets of Croydon and, when people shouted racist abuse, they held hands tighter. On the day Samuel died, he bought her some of her favourite snowball chrysanthemums just before going to the station (Jessie makes a point of saying, in *her* book, that those chrysanthemums were for her). And it was little Gwendolyn who answered the door when he stumbled home after fainting at West Croydon Station. "No one saw me," he told her. The tragedy of her father being ignored, of nobody helping when he fell, would haunt her for years. As he died he called to her, but Jessie bustled the children out of the house to stay with a friend.

Afterwards, when Gwendolyn cycled three and a half miles to school, she always arrived late because she went by way of Bandon Hill Cemetery where her father was buried. In her teens when she sang "Spring Had Come" from *Hiawatha* at the Regal Cinema, Brighton, to her brother's conducting, she fell in love with the flautist Joe Slater. Her mother took Joe aside, lied to him that Gwendolyn would die if she had children and sent him away. After a marriage her mother did approve of, which ultimately proved unworkable, Gwendolyn got a divorce, changed her name to Avril for a fresh start and started composing and conducting in earnest, writing an orchestral composition entitled, appropriately, *To April*, which she conducted herself in 1929. She moved to a flat in St John's Wood near her friends; composer Joseph Holbrooke, operatic baritone, healer and Mohawk Chief Os Ke Non Ton, who often invited her "for a meal of grass and nuts"[1] and Minnie Aumonier, who lived nearby in Temple Fortune Lane.

She wrote some of her larger works under the name of Peter Riley, but she also had excellent notices in the papers under her own name. Her piano concerto, which premiered in Aberdeen in 1941 under her own conducting – how I long to know if she used the baton presented to her father in America, made of cedar from the home of Frederick Douglass – got rave reviews. "Strangely unfeminine in its make-up, but it displays the fine melodic gifts which Miss Coleridge-Taylor has inherited from her father."[2]

Dressmaker for the Royal Family, Norman Hartnell, designed white gowns for her, to show Avril in dramatic silhouette and feminine contrast as she conducted RAF choirs during the war, the Royal Marines in Hyde Park or the black-clad London Symphony Orchestra in the Albert Hall. But she wanted to prove to herself that her compositions and conducting would stand on their own merits, not as the conducting and composing of the daughter of Samuel Coleridge-Taylor. So, she found one country that hadn't heard of him: South Africa.

And there, she was a great success, broadcasting with the SABC Symphony. She fell in love with the "colour, music, laughter and gaiety, flowers, sunsets and dawn skies unsurpassed"[3], and, of course, she was treated as white. She felt guilty about this; her father had written many furious letters against racism in British newspapers, but she didn't feel she had the right to interfere with someone else's politics and believed that, if she could stay, she might get to a position where she could effect change from within. She sold up in London and moved permanently to South Africa, composing a "Comet Prelude" while on the inaugural flight of the first jet air liner service in 1952. The flight was well-documented in the papers, as were its select passengers. The international press announced that the daughter of Samuel Coleridge-Taylor was to conduct the Cape Town Symphony, had a commission to write the music for a three-act ballet to be produced by the Ballet Society in Johannesburg and was to give a series of broadcasts for Springbok Radio.

Perhaps it was this publicity that finally made the South African authorities aware of her racial heritage. All offers of work evaporated and she faced serious destitution. She came back to England without having composed the ballet. In 1956, she formed a choir in London called the New World Singers, made up of people from the West Indies, many of them part of the recent Windrush-era wave of migration. One of the tenors sang her song "I Can Face it, Lord" for the BBC. In the following year, she wrote the Ghanaian Independence March.

Then she fell into a depression and never composed again.

Can sorrow find one, even hidden in a mist of blue forget-me-nots? Avril's son said: "In the music world mother was discriminated against more as a coloured woman than as a woman."[4]

But I feel that another reason for the neglect of Amanda and Avril's music is the problem that affects many of the other women in my sheet music collection: they wrote tunes on the brink of an era when serious composers didn't write tunes anymore. Black or white, it was the dogma coming from the acolytes of Schoenberg, expressed by Charles Wuorinen in 1979 when he stated that tonal music is "no longer employed by serious composers of the mainstream".

Avril was, for a time, curator of the Colt Clavier Collection of historical keyboard instruments in Bethersden, Kent. She lived on-site in a little house with cats she rescued from RSPCA shelters named Pizzicato, Tutti, Minim, Crotchet and Quaver. She died in a nursing home in Seaford in 1998.

Listening to Avril

Avril Coleridge-Taylor is not unknown; there are articles about her here and there, she is mentioned in some dictionaries of women composers, and she only died in 1998. Amanda Aldridge, in her unmarked grave in Streatham Park Cemetery, seemed, of the two, most needful of remembrance.

But when I went to the British Library Sound Archive to listen to Avril's works, they were still on old tapes, waiting for someone, anyone, to apply for them to be digitised and made accessible.

After three months, two requests and a nag, it was finally done. I had a whole booth to myself for the entire day, with Avril in my ears. For the first hour, it was just talking; much of it was interviews. Her clipped, deliberate speech bore witness to her elocution lessons at the Trinity School of Music, where she'd also studied piano, violin, dancing and singing. In interview after interview, she is asked about her father, Samuel Coleridge-Taylor. His life story, his works, her memories of him. At last, on a show broadcast on the BBC's West African Regional Programme, the interviewer finally says, "Let us now talk about you" – a slight pause – "what do you think of your father's music?"

After a while, he does come round to her own compositions and asks her if it's true that she composes under a pseudonym. "Yes," she affirms. "But I don't intend to tell you what it is." The interviewers are uninspired. When Avril says, "I enjoy listening to pop music and have a number of favourite tunes," she is not asked to name them.

As I went through the newly-digitised files, each one named perfunctorily by those sorting out the BBC archives in the 1970s, I found that the music in the collection was not Avril's but Samuel's. What I'd thought was her piece for violin and piano, marked tantalisingly op. 7, was in fact her father's Ballade in C minor op. 73. What I'd been told was Avril Coleridge-Taylor's Symphonic Variations was from my memory the Symphonic Variations on an African Air op. 63 by Samuel Coleridge-Taylor. Avril was the conductor. Though in this 1942 live recording, and also in a recording of her father's "Othello March" from 1938 it was clear that Avril was an excellent conductor. The music, hardly core repertoire for orchestras, was performed with brisk, authoritative clarity – energetic, building beautifully as it went, a great sense of structure. Most annoyingly, the file of her Windrush-immigrant choir, The New World Singers, performing her arrangement of "Were You There When They Crucified My Lord" turned out to be a cuckoo's egg containing Samuel's "Hiawatha's Wedding Feast".

From a "Ballad Concert" in 1936 we have the multi-talented Avril singing "Oh What Comes" from her father's Sorrow Songs, "This is the Island of Gardens" from his Songs of Sun and Shade and, for a change, the Irish song I Know Where I'm Going with its phrase "Some say he's black/But I say he's bonny." Her voice is a pleasant fluttery soprano of the kind favoured by the English in the 1930s, very well trained. The diction is clear as a bell.

Late in the afternoon, I finally got to hear her compositional voice. "Today being Ghana's National Day, we begin the programme with the Ghana Ceremonial March by Avril Coleridge-Taylor," says the announcer. Then came a virile opening fanfare with plenty of drum, which launched into a complex, restless march, questing round several interesting chords and unexpected, clashing bass notes, far more adventurous and quirky than the usual tub-thumper that is written for such occasions. It was more like film music. In one of the earlier interviews she'd said of this march that she wanted to "convey the feeling of triumph … on the achievement of their independence" and that she had given a private recording of the piano version of it to Dr Nkrumah, the prime minister, whom she'd met in London earlier. In the same interview, she said in her deliberate and precisely-enunciated way that "after all, music is an expression of thoughts and feelings. Music is also an expression of spiritual meaning."

There was a less scripted interview with one Paddy Bell on Springbok Radio's "Pan American Clipper Club of the Air", a weekly feature interviewing someone notable who had just arrived in Johannesburg. There is no date on it. Paddy, an American, had clearly researched her well, and mentions her father and his famous work, "Hiawatha". He asks if it would suit an open air performance in South Africa. I felt a strange quiver go through the headphones, and I realised I was imagining her shock at no longer being her own person in her newly-adopted country. She recovers, explaining the necessity of having an acoustic shell for an orchestra and choir outdoors, and then reflects that it might be a beautiful thing: " … you have the birds." She comes across as a lovely person throughout. I left the booth wondering if the avuncular Paddy had sealed her fate.

The Refuge and Reform of Caroline Sheridan Norton

Forms I have loved, – as bright
As in life's joyous years;
Say not 'tis dark! – the murkiest night
Hath light enough for tears.

from "Say Not 'Tis Dark" – Caroline Sheridan Norton
(*The Sorrows of Rosalie*, 1829)

IN 2016, THE Houses of Parliament hosted a "Suffragette Season" and Andrea and I were lucky enough to be asked to perform, after a few famous speakers, for a themed banquet in one of the grand, gold-and-green flocked rooms. We eagerly brought along the music, put Andrea's electric piano and our velvet dresses through the X-ray machines, were issued with passes and nearly tripped over ourselves gazing at the beauty of the building, both the spiky exterior and the rich-toned interior.

By the time we were ushered into the banquet room, the guests – an association to do with historic buildings – were very well-oiled indeed.

I planned to say a little bit about the composers, and was particularly keen to mention Caroline Sheridan, known by her husband's name, Norton. I wanted to make the walls ring with her lovely melodies, so seldom performed today, and then tell the banqueters that these songs and poems were by a talented woman whose energies and imagination turned personal tragedy and injustice into some of the most important legal reforms to affect women in the Victorian era.

I didn't even try. The loud guffaws, the networking, the braying into mobile phones were difficult to sing against, let alone speak against. Andrea played the piano she'd had to haul from her three gigs in Yorkshire that day, but she might as well not have bothered; I sang, but I was no match for this hubbub. Even when we came

Caroline Sheridan, known by her husband's name, Norton, was accused of being a "she-devil" but was actually only guilty of marrying a sadistic, petty man.

to Dame Ethel Smyth's "March of the Women" where, as planned, costumed re-enactors joined us, two men next to our platform just shouted louder into their phones, and the booming laughter in the corner continued.

On our confused way out of the maze, we passed a marble bust of Lord Melbourne. He looked a bit uneasy, his blank eyes looking vaguely off into the distance, some way past his right shoulder. I was suddenly glad of the way the performance had turned out. I was able, in some weird, tiny – *very* tiny – way, to walk in the shoes of Lady Caroline Norton.

There are quite a number of books on Caroline Sheridan Norton. *A Scandalous Woman, The Criminal Conversation of Mrs Norton,*

Caroline Norton's Defense; with titles like that, one expects to find orgies, opium, ménages a trois, quatre, six...

For someone called a "she-devil", a "she-beast" and of whom the *British and Foreign Review* asked, "And can *she* be a wife and a mother?", the sins of Caroline Sheridan Norton are – well, there aren't any. Like so many women of her time, she was afraid of being condemned to spinsterhood and married a sadistic, petty, dull man who felt threatened by her talents and intellect, and who was of an opposite political persuasion.

She was admired and had many important friends including William, 2nd Viscount Melbourne, who had known her famous grandfather, playwright Richard Brinsley Sheridan. Her husband encouraged her to entertain Melbourne; he wanted a government job and thought the old boy would succumb to feminine persuasion. Melbourne duly made him magistrate for Whitechapel, but Norton started to feel jealous, and named Lord Melbourne, then the Prime Minister of Great Britain, as co-respondent in a "criminal conversation" suit. The press had as much of a field day then as they would now. Caroline was found to be innocent, but while Melbourne's reputation – he was already famous for being cuckolded by Lord Byron – benefited by his association with the younger woman, hers was ruined. And she was separated from her beloved children.

Unlike her friend, author Mary Shelley, Caroline Sheridan Norton did not campaign for equal rights for women. In the 1830s, society was so cruelly unjust that change had to come bit by painstaking bit. All Caroline asked for was the right to see her children and the right to have access to her own inheritance, earnings and belongings.

In the biographies of Caroline Sheridan Norton, men's names crop up again and again. The brilliant friends she invited to her dinner parties, such as Thomas Moore of *Moore's Melodies*, known for "Believe Me If All Those Endearing Young Charms" and "The Minstrel Boy"; the inventor – with Ada Lovelace – of the first computer, mathematician Charles Babbage; novelist Harrison Ainsworth; dandy-novelist Edward Bulwer-Lytton; the young politician Benjamin Disraeli; and a list of other politicians that

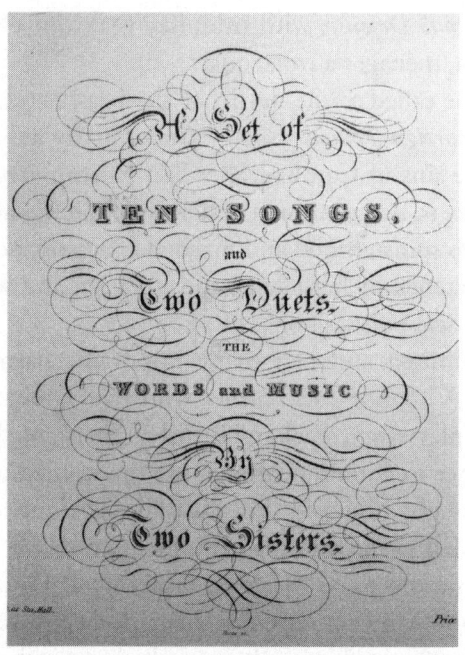

Caroline and her sister Helen collaborated on A Set of Ten Songs and Two Duets, writing alternate songs and becoming ever more sorrowful as they progress.

would cause most readers to skip this paragraph out of the boredom that would surely ensue. Many biographers speak of her need to befriend, flirt with and be charming to men. Alan Chedzoy, author of *A Scandalous Woman*, speaks of the time after her public shaming: "With the exceptions of her mother and sisters, Caroline had never before thought of cultivating friendship among other women."[1]

When I went to the British Library to research Caroline, it was one nasty thing after another. The countless horrendous stories about her husband scalding her with boiling water, setting things on fire, shoving her down a flight of stairs and causing her to miscarry, the humiliating trial full of innuendo and mocking laughter, Lord Melbourne ignoring her pleas for help and support; the satirical drawings in the press, insults hurled at her by the newspapers, and her inability, as a woman, to sue; the way her own money was kept from her by her husband, her children crying for "Mama!" when she tried to come and visit them, her husband's mistress slamming the door to her, the death of her middle son left riding unsupervised, a badly-washed wound causing tetanus while she was prevented from having any contact with them; it is unpleasant and unrelenting. Even her biographers seem keen to criticize; Jane Gray Perkins in 1909 saying: "I have made no attempt to disguise Mrs Norton's faults or magnify her virtues, or to defend her beyond the point when defence becomes special pleading."[2]

And then I came to the oldest books I'd signed out. Suddenly, in a large, calm expanse of creamy paper with a printing block indent round the edges like the banks of an ornamental pond, in swirling clouds of calligraphic flourishes are the words *A Set of Ten Songs and Two Duets, The Words and Music by Two Sisters*.

Peaceful, beautiful, and because it was music, private. Caroline Sheridan Norton is remembered first as a campaigner, second as a writer, third as a beauty, but her songs are a footnote, an appendix.

Caroline and her sister Helen alternate contributions. The first is by Helen, "H.S.B.", and it is a sad song. "They bid me forget thee, they tell me that now/The grave damp is staining that beautiful brow." The next one, by Caroline, is "But Thou!" about unrequited love. Helen's next one is "Oh Sing No More That Saddening Strain", which is ironic because the sisters seem to vie with each other to write ever more sorrowful songs with the next seven, "The Change", "The Mother's Lament", "Chactas' Lament for Atala", "The Land I Love" ("'twere a wasted life that was not spent beside thee"), "Bygone Hours" and "I Have Left My Quiet Home". The two duets aren't much more cheerful. The last is called "To-morrow" and includes the lines: "Harsh fate has made your bloom to fade, you may not smile tomorrow; That idol form may feed the worm and fill the grave tomorrow."

The tunes themselves are mostly in the major key, which presents a picture of elegant resignation; powerless to change any of it, one might as well play the piano and smile. I found more songs and warmed to them. It was in these ditties I finally found a vividly tangible female presence.

Among the "Set of Twelve Songs Written, composed and dedicated to the Countess of Jersey by Mrs Price Blackwood and The Hon Mrs. Norton" are "And I Have Lost Thee", "I Am Weary", "How Sad it is,

The Lonely Harp" and "I Do Not Love Thee". There is also "A Set of Seven Songs and a duet by the Hon Mrs Norton" with a small notice below that Chappell is "Music Seller to Her Majesty and to HRH the Duchess of Kent" and that one might also purchase more works by Mrs Norton and her sister, and also "All the songs composed by Mrs Robert Arkwright" Not a male composer in sight.

More women – friends and relatives – appeared in the dedications to the songs. "Inscribed to The Lady Emmeline Stuart Wortley", "Inscribed to the Hon Mrs Leicester Stanhope," "Affectionately Inscribed to Mrs Brinsley Sheridan", "Affectionately Inscribed to the Rt Hon Lady Seymour", "Inscribed to Mrs T Delves Broughton". Augusta Cowell's name comes up repeatedly. She collaborated with Caroline many times, writing the music for "An Indian Exile", "The Midshipman" and "The Lonely Harp". The *Athenaeum* in 1833 admires Cowell's melody for "We Have Been Friends Together" calling her "an illustrious obscure". She's still obscure now. It took a bit of digging to find that she was a spinster at the time, living with her mother and brother near Hyde Park. About a decade later, in 1849, when she was 48, she married a twice-widowed rector with 11 children. Despite having spent significant time with Caroline, and doubtless helping her through some terrible days, she's barely mentioned in biographies and doesn't show up at all in the index of *A Scandalous Woman*.

The cloistered world of these aristocrats and non-professionals ensured that music was kept under wraps, a refuge, a private activity and even when it was published, it was still virtually in code. It seems almost understood that only another woman in another hushed withdrawing-room had the power to unlock a song. In the 1860s, poor Claribel had been pilloried for the commercial success of her cheerful ditties, but Norton and her friends were almost left alone with their charming songs; they weren't political pamphlets, after all. When I looked into the names behind the songs, however, I found some surprising stories.

Her Grace the Duchess of Sutherland, to whom Caroline dedicated "The Blind Girl" (refrain: "Dark, dark forever is my earthy home"), campaigned against slavery. A frequently cited reference to her is a mean-spirited piece of writing by Karl Marx, pointing out what he saw as hypocrisy in the duchess' campaigning activities: "The history of the Sutherland family is the history of the ruin and expropriation of the Scotch-Gaelic people … My Lady Countess had people burned in their huts."[3] Though "My Lady Countess" was not the anti-slavery Harriett, Duchess of Sutherland, but her mother-in-law. Harriett Sutherland started many philanthropic causes, knew prison reformer Elizabeth Fry and was Queen Victoria's mistress of the robes. For weeks after Prince Albert died, she was the only person permitted to comfort the distraught Queen. She also stood by Caroline after the trial when the majority of society shunned her, and took her riding in her open carriage.

Lady Mary Fox, born FitzClarence, dedicatee of the song "We Are the Wandering Breezes", was the illegitimate daughter of William IV and his mistress Dorothea Jordan. Her royal father could not give her his name, but left her the "Anthony Roll", a priceless set of illustrations of King Henry VIII's ships. She was housekeeper of Windsor Castle for her reigning cousin, and wrote a utopian fantasy called *Account of an Expedition to the Interior of New Holland* which satirises the convict system, portraying an Australia where the remote tribes run an enlightened, and rather feminist, society.

Compassion is what marks many of these ladies out. Compassion and an almost sensual thrill, and joy in, morbid stories. Lady Emmeline Stuart-Wortley, dedicatee of "The Song of the Fairies" ("Sleep, mortal, sleep" goes its refrain, before you think we've finally arrived at a happy song) was, along with Caroline Sheridan Norton, an editor of fashionable journals such as *The Keepsake* and *La Belle Assemblee and Court*. Domestic, disposable and ornamental, these journals included poetry, reproductions of engravings, stories and bits of travel reportage. When I ordered a copy of *La Belle Assemblee* produced under Caroline's editorship, the British Library discovered it had been burned in the Blitz. They changed their records and referred me to a scanned version courtesy of the Karlsruhe Institut für Technologie.

I read it until my eyes ached. Miss JA Porter tells of when, as a child, she was on board the Sir Godfrey Webster when Gothic author MG Lewis died after "pacing up and down the deck and spouting forth Italian and German poetry in a wild and impassioned tone of voice". She recounts his body refusing to sink when it was thrown overboard. In "The Pilgrim" she gives us the tale of a penitent daughter of a Marchese walking barefoot, an old lady and known murderess speaking of the barefoot woman's sins and, later, a general dancing in the street while another young woman's body was borne by six priests singing a requiem, a white rose between the corpse's lips. Emmeline Stuart Wortley, a fellow journal editor, gives us a harrowing poem about the wreck of the Rothesay Castle steamboat in 1831. Also present and contributing is "Anne of Swansea," really Ann Julia Kemble Curtis Hatton, sister of Sarah Siddons and aunt of Caroline Norton's close friend and defender, Fanny Kemble. Anne was regularly published by Minerva Press; Gothic novels a speciality – *Secrets in Every Mansion, Secret Avengers* and *Guilty or Not Guilty* to name only three. For *La Belle Assemblee*, she shares a poem, the melancholic and beautiful "Lines Addressed to Mary".

I'd always been unmoved when learning about the problems of those living in grand houses. Reading Jane Austen as a teenager, I'd throw the book down in disgust; her characters had servants and dancing lessons and didn't have to do the shivering, hard labour of the majority of the world's people. Their problems seemed tiny. But the tender, almost coded life that these ladies had through their sad songs and gently tragic magazines gave me a different perspective. The female realm of the Gothic – dungeons, keys, veils, walls, darkness, moats and curses – revealed itself as the slightly more morbid sister of the genteel parlour ballad. Both forms being a natural form of expression to those with an education, but no existence in law. "I do not ask for my rights. I have no rights; I have only wrongs,"[4] Caroline Sheridan Norton said in court as her husband and his lawyers bullied her. The phrase would not be out of place in the mouth of a heroine of Gothic fiction. Even the most magnificent dungeon is still a dungeon. Tuneful ditties resonate eerily against their walls, making those within more human.

Caroline eventually changed the law. She charmed a lot of men, acting coquettish when she knew it would help her cause. She picked her battles, publicly saying that she did not want to have equal rights, only what she called natural rights. In a letter to Mary Shelley, she revealed her true feelings in a bit of gentle ribbing, describing the fairer sex as "whom you have not the clever woman's affectation of thinking inferior to men". She highlighted the irony of married women being virtually invisible under a female sovereign in a letter to Queen Victoria, which was published and reprinted many times (its full title being *A Letter to the Queen on Lord Chancellor Cranworth's Marriage and Divorce Bill*). She campaigned tirelessly, working with politicians inclined to sympathise with her, facing abuse from those who objected to what they saw as her interference in their world and writing pamphlets, letters, novels and poems to support her cause.

Along the way, she managed to get her surviving two children back, and it was when one was ill that she wrote her most popular song-hit "Juanita" *(CD track 25)*. Her son Brinsley, whose guitar she wrote it for, took the message to heart and scandalised his father and London society by marrying an illiterate daughter of a Capri fisherman. By all accounts, it was a happy marriage.

Caroline's friend Emmeline Stuart-Wortley's husband died in 1844, prompting her to leave her cloister to explore America, Mexico, Havana, Panama, Jamaica, Portugal and Madeira. Unfortunately, she suffered a leg fracture from a mule's kick in Lebanon and died of dysentery between Antioch and Beirut in 1855. Her other chum, Lady Mary Fox, astonished her friends by selling the precious Anthony Roll to the British Museum in 1858. She wanted the money for good works.

Finally, in 1857 the Matrimonial Causes Act was passed by Parliament. That year, there were three divorce petitions in England and Wales. The following year, there were three hundred. By then, Caroline's first triumph, the Custody of Children Act, had been permitting separated and divorced women access to their own children for almost twenty years. Then at long last, the Women's Property Act was passed in 1870. George Norton died in 1875, and in 1877, Caroline Sheridan Norton enjoyed the matrimonial bliss that had so long been denied her, marrying politician and art historian Sir William Stirling-Maxwell on the 1st of March. She died three months later.

Andrea and I were in the wrong part of the Houses of Parliament that night. If we'd strayed as far as the gilded chamber of the House of Lords, we might have seen the fresco facing the sovereign's throne, depicting a dark-haired Justice, her features strong and calm. The model was Caroline Sheridan Norton, campaigner, author, poet and composer of parlour songs.

India By Way of a Parlour Piano (and the North Circular)

FOR YEARS, THE piano was considered a lady's instrument. A lady could be seated at a piano with her knees together and her head bent modestly to the keys, eyelashes fluttering. Playing a piano did not involve positioning anything between her legs and, God forbid, it did not involve blowing. Caroline Watts' "Bugler Girl" on the National Union of Women's Suffrage Society's posters was deliberately provocative. Barefoot, legs sturdily apart, a sword at her side, a bugle in her mouth and making a loud, strenuous noise. Pianos were so much nicer. So effeminate was the piano that Victorian teacher and composer John Hullah wrote that, when Oxford University saw the first public performance of a male pianist in 1827, he was greeted with "a storm of hisses"[1]. Pianos at that time were carefully-crafted luxuries, each going through the hands of dozens of craftspeople. Then, in the 1880s, standardisation made it possible for companies to buy pre-made components and assemble cheap uprights for the young ladies of middle-class and even – good God – working-class households. Army & Navy Stores sold them on a hire-purchase basis. Even Harrods went after the less well-off, offering second-hand instruments on monthly payments. Rich and aristocratic daughters started to turn to the violin instead, as their privileged accomplishments were no longer so exclusive.

Looking through joke books from the 1900s, I noticed early the archetype of the girl piano student. She was always the butt of the joke. I remember my English grandfather favouring me with one of these jokes, very archly saying:

"So, the girl says to her teacher, 'Am I sitting too far away from the piano?' and he replies, oh, my *dear* girl…" I interrupted: "Yeah, yeah, something like, 'you can *never* sit too far from the piano'. Yeah, yeah." He looked crestfallen; I'd been rude, but I was angry. The piano was an important place of escape. I believed already at that age that everyone should have that place.

When I was rehearsing the songs for this project with Andrea early in 2017, she came along to our flat for dinner afterwards. Nowadays, artistic activities in London rarely take one into the centre; one must travel around the cheaper, outlying parts. In this case, Andrea, who lives in Charlton, was driving her car from rehearsal in South Tottenham to my place in Hanwell, a semicircle of thirty-five miles.

We passed the J Reid Piano Factory, a splendid Georgian frontage on St Ann's Road. This was fascinating to see because I had just learned that Tottenham and Harringay used to be filled with piano manufacturers, obtaining their wood from barges going up the River Lea, the iron for their frames from local foundries, and their mechanisms from craftsmen based in Camden. Just a ten-minute walk from J Reid, Challen Pianos once made instruments for the BBC and constructed "The largest piano in the world" for the silver jubilee of King George V in 1935. Urban legend has it that it then went to an aristocratic family up north who used it for garden party entertainments, where it sank into the boggy damp ground, too heavy to sit on moist earth. The one I'd learnt on was a small, dark upright.

I remembered reading in an old Steinway advert that a piano assists children "through their most difficult times to a sane and beautiful life". Andrea commented that she might well use that for her piano-teaching business, Piano Maestros.

"It's true," she said. "Learning music has that power."

"Absolutely. I'd come home from horrible school and play the music that made me feel farthest away from it, like 'The Temple Bells'. Not only was I in India, I was in 1905," I said. "It took me to a beautiful life in my head."

Andrea said: "For me, learning to read music was like mathematics at school. I found that by using my brain I could make art."

"So, was it an escape?"

"No, it was an immersion."

"If 'The Temple Bells' was my escape, what did you immerse yourself in?"

"I played the whole of the Anna Magdalena Bach book. We only had one of the pieces in the state-issued piano book in Slovakia, and I went and found the rest."

At that moment, we were going through Wembley. The 2007 stadium, with its design of a semicircle of scaffolding arching into the air, made me favour poor Andrea with my usual monologue about the British Empire Exhibition Stadium and its rounded towers, and all the miscellaneous bits of plaster I came across wandering around the site in 2002, newly arrived from Canada and determined to visit as many Great Exhibition sites as possible, even if it was just a few crumbling lions' heads with grass growing in the cracks. But what was most interesting to relate was the fact that of all the pavilions in 1924's British Empire Exhibition – East Africa, Ceylon, "Burmah", Nigeria, British Guyana, Canada, South Africa and others – one of the largest was India, and it was the only one whose in-house music was dominated by women.

"In fact," I said, "'The Temple Bells' was actually played here in Wembley!"

We turned down Ealing Road. "This is much more Indian than 'The Temple Bells' or probably that exhibition," Andrea commented as we went past the Shri Vallabh Nidhi temple, sand-coloured and intricate, and beyond it the shops selling bolts of purple and gold cloth and box upon box of mangos.

"Certainly. And I'll bet if Amy and Liza had been alive at the time, they wouldn't have approved of their fake-Indian pieces being used to represent the country itself."

Amy Woodforde-Finden had written her set of *Four Indian Love Lyrics* just over two decades before the exhibition in Wembley, and "The Temple Bells" was the first of the four. These *Love Lyrics*, and Liza Lehmann's *Persian Garden* cycle constituted a genteel English Parlour version of the exotic Raj, and as such were featured heavily in the Indian Pavilion in 1924.

Lehmann was the first president of the Society of Women Musicians, and *In a Persian Garden,* her 1896 song-cycle to selections from Omar Khayyam's *Rubaiyat* was probably her most successful work. It was rejected by publishers and only printed as a personal favour to a powerful friend of hers, Angelina "Channa" Goetz (née Levy) and mother-in-law to her sister Alma, who promised to host the first performances at her London home. From there, it blazed its way through parlours in London, the UK, America and the rest of

Liza Lehmann found married life more conducive to composing than that of a touring singer. In 1911 she became the first president of the Society of Women Musicians.

the world. Lehmann had never been to Asia or the Middle East and said in her memoirs that any local colour came to her instinctively or "emanated from the spirit of the poem". She was fond of quoting a young lady who rushed up after a performance to say: "The local colour is *too* wonderful – I simply felt as if I was at *Liberty's*!"[2]

The sheet music itself was as lovely as a piece of Liberty fabric. Metzler and Co took pains to produce an edition with the title framed by a Moorish arch, crammed full of swirling stylised arabesques of peonies and carnations in light yellow and pale blue.

It was this sort of artwork on the covers of old music that drew me to them when I was a young girl. Antiques were beautiful, their detailed workmanship, carving, metal filigree, burnished patina, glowing enamel and waxed mahogany sending thrills through my body. I could afford none of it, but I could find a few dimes to buy old sheet music, usually in a pile of ephemera near the books section of any charity shop. As my mum looked for clothes for the family, I went straight to the books corner, and if there was a new stack of tattered sheet music, my hands would start to tremble.

This was how I first came across *In a Persian Garden*, and also Woodforde-Finden's *Four Indian Love Lyrics (CD tracks 27-30)*.

These *Love Lyrics* were my favourites. Not only was the cover gorgeous, a sensually grainy lithograph in greens, yellows, pinks, blues and reds of a woman in a sari carrying an earthenware jug on her head, surrounded by palm trees and about to dip her toes into a lake filled with waterlilies, but also the songs were playable. They got their effect of exoticism very simply, very directly. In one bar, I could be somewhere far, far away.

The *Four Indian Love Lyrics* were composed in 1903 by Amy (Amelia) Woodforde-Finden. The words were written by Laurence Hope, whose real name was Adela Florence Nicolson, née Cory. They were born five years apart, Amelia Ward in Chile and Adela Cory just north of Bristol. Both married officers of the Raj, Amy in 1894 to Lieutenant Colonel Woodforde-Finden of the Bengal Medical Service, and Adela in 1889 to Colonel Malcolm Nicolson of the Bombay Army. Adela was a fluent linguist, having edited the *Civil & Military Gazette* in Lahore with her father and, after her marriage, she joined her husband on the North West Frontier disguised as a Pashtun boy, speaking Urdu, riding horses and sleeping rough. Among the other Raj wives, she was considered outrageously eccentric. Violet Jacob, writer and poet married to an Irish major based in Mhow, described her in 1897 as "a very strange woman, vilely and impossibly clothed ... of course everyone mocks at her".[3] Nicolson herself wrote: "Men should be judged not by their tint of skin, the gods they serve, the vintage that they drink ... but by the quality of thought they think."[4] And thus she and her husband welcomed a wide multi-ethnic, multi-caste group of friends to their home. As she wrote in "Song of the Parao":

> *These are my people, and this my land,*
> *I hear the voice of her secret soul.*
> *This is the life that I understand,*
> *Savage and simple and sane and whole.*[5]

She disguised her writing by using a pseudonym, pretending that a lot of it was simply translation and not original (a fiction still perpetuated on the internet at the time of writing). The reactions were mixed. A critic in London panted: "Mr Hope (sic) has caught admirably the dominant notes of this Indian love poetry ... the hot scented jungle", whereas an Indian writer in the *Calcutta Review* was having none of it, saying Hope was one of those writers "who has made 'opportunity' of India, in a way we cannot but resent ... sheltering behind a misrepresentation of a country their knowledge of which may be summed up in the bare fact that it is the home of elemental passion ... illicit, unlawful loves ... gross are the details". The *Garden of Kama* was a wild hit in drawing rooms, despite another warning from *The Reader* in 1902 saying the work would "make the respectable squirm in holy disgust" before adding "it is very much better that people should be shocked into attention, rather than that they should not attend at all".

The fact that the lusts depicted in the poems were from another culture put them at a remove. *The Garden of Kama* was perhaps a racy book for a young woman to have in her collection or to be seen reading, but it wouldn't ruin her reputation.

When Amy Woodforde-Finden set some of the verses to music in 1901, she added another layer of exoticism with her use of "oriental" modal harmonies and throbbing repetitions of chords and fifths. Richness, octaves, dynamic contrasts; she turned the intensity of "Less than the Dust" up a notch by building to a vocal climax on the words "Farewell, Zahirudin", then repeating the name, "Za-hi-ru-din" and fading away, as if the singer is falling to the ground, bleeding to death. All playable by a beginner-intermediate level pianist with an easy vocal range.

Initially, Amy couldn't find a publisher either. She printed the four songs at her own expense in 1902 and they proved so popular amongst the sexy new Edwardians that Boosey and Co repented its decision and made her a handsome offer. As the *Radio Times* said in 1924: "If sales are any criterion of popularity, the most popular songs ever published in the history of music are the *Indian Love Lyrics*."

The most well-known of the four songs by far was the "Kashmiri Love Song", popularly known as "Pale Hands I Loved Beside the

Amy Woodforde-Finden captivated restless young Edwardian women with her musical evocations of exotic cultures.

Shalimar". This song and its verse inspired films, novels, plays, two perfumes – Dubarry's Garden of Kama in 1919 and Guerlain's Shalimar in 1925, still available today – and a 1937 nail varnish called Pale Hands Pink Tipped. Rudolph Valentino recorded the song and it was also performed by the Whittall Rug Company's jazz band, the Anglo Persians, given ragtime versions, swing versions, made into a foxtrot, a waltz and was still being used in muzak recordings in the 1970s for malls and elevators. Though even Amy Woodforde-Finden must have found some of Adela's poem too strong, omitting the verse that went, "How the hot blood rushed wildly through the veins/Beneath your touch", just as she left out the "bridal bed" stanza from "The Temple Bells".

"The Temple Bells" used a device as effective as it was simple: the left hand beat a slow, Arabic "Malfouf" rhythm in fifths through the entire song. The right hand beat the same rhythm, but added a grace note that was both a flirtatious tickle and a little jolt of urgency. It was as if the parlour upright could become a wardrobe to Narnia for every well-brought-up young girl kept within the confines of a respectable house. I knew, with my hands, the secret of those young Edwardian women.

"Escapist tosh for Victorian girls," my father called it once. "It's all a bit too much," said my mother. I played it louder.

The next time I went to Vancouver for the day, I visited the big public library to find something out about the woman who had written the music. I was gratified to discover Amy's adventures and travels were not made up or created as an "escape". It was a gift from her own life. I squealed with delight when I read that Laurence Hope was a woman. Her verses were an expression of passions that she lived. But in 1904, after her husband died during a prostate operation, she killed herself by swallowing perchloride of mercury. Thomas Hardy wrote her obituary in the *Atheneaum* and her son Malcolm was left to edit her final volume, *Indian Love*, with its suicide-note dedication that ends: "Small joy was I to thee; before we met/Sorrow had left thee all too sad to save./Useless my love – as vain as this regret/That pours my hopeless life across thy grave."

Since then, the Indian writer and feminist Kamala Das has counted her as an inspiration and her quotes are now shared on social media.

Woodforde-Finden wrote many more song cycles, all with exotic titles: *Myrtles of Damascus, The Pagoda of Flowers, Stars of the Desert, Five Japanese Songs, A Dream of Egypt* and even a set of *Mexican Songs*. She set many different poets, including "In a Latticed Balcony" by the Indian freedom fighter and suffragist Sarojini Naidu, whom the *New Republic* in 1916 compared unfavourably with Adela Nicolson/Laurence Hope, complaining that there was "nothing specially Hindoo" about Naidu's verses. Rumours still lurk in the archives of national newspapers that Amy and Adela met in India, Amy played Adela the *Love Lyrics* and they plunged into a passionate but doomed and short-lived love affair.

Sarojini Naidu, the Nightingale of India. After the Amritsar massacre in 1919, she stopped writing poetry and turned to politics.

Amy Woodforde-Finden died a year after Liza Lehmann in 1919, while seated at her piano bench working on another song. Half a decade after their deaths, Lehmann's *In a Persian Garden* and Woodforde-Finden's *Four Indian Love Lyrics* were played at the India Pavilion at the British Empire Exhibition in Wembley. Two women as wrongly, bizarrely white as the plaster lions but opening up a world through their pianos.

Something Other

GROWING UP IN a community founded by loggers less than a century before, the highest meaningful praise I could be given was that I was like a boy. Building, driving, lifting, demolishing; important things weren't done in the house. Being 'like a girl' was a flat out insult; at best it could mean a tendency to pink and lace, at worst an inability to do big things. The "something other" had not been identified, and could not be commended.

I feel it is the same in the study of music history. It is harder to understand the nebulous, intimate, often strange atmosphere that distinguishes many of the songs women wrote, but there is some kind of message being spelled out in the words and music contained in these pieces of sheet music; gradually forming around me over the years. Is it a strange freedom, a quirkiness, an unaccustomed directness from women who were, musically, outside of the system? It is still clouded to me, each song showing shapes through the mist.

Marjorie Pickthall's biographer and anthologist Lorne Pierce lists what he regards as the Canadian poet's strengths and weaknesses: "On the one hand there are grace and charm, a restrained Christian mysticism, and unfailing cadence; on the other, preoccupation with the unearthly, with death and regret, with loneliness and grief."[1] Critic Desmond Pacey is less kind: "Knowing little of the world of men and affairs, she was compelled to draw her inspiration from books, and about all her work there is a bookish, indoor atmosphere."[2] Tellingly, he continues, in the *University of Toronto Quarterly* in 1931 that "revery is only second-hand vision and, like hearsay, only partially convincing; it is a truism that the greatest art is the product of direct vision". If a preoccupation with loneliness and grief is considered a weakness, then a great many English Lit courses need an immediate revamp. Reverie and the "indoor atmosphere" is an integral part of life. And the indirect can be enormously effective.

Take Alma Goetz's "Mélisande in the Wood" *(CD track 31).* This is a small song, barely two minutes long, for one singer and a piano, and yet it has mysterious depths, a presence like a ghost. Ethel Clifford's words are powerful. In Maeterlinck's symbolist play, Mélisande is a victim whose tragic fate is clear from the outset. Found grieving in a forest with her crown sunk in a pool, she tells Prince Goulad not to touch her, but he takes her away and makes her marry him and live in a festering castle where she eventually dies in childbirth. She doesn't have much to say for herself in the play, but Clifford's poem gives us more insight in three short stanzas than Maeterlinck provides for her in five acts. There is a lingering over darkness, fluids and heavy resignation at powerlessness here, which Clifford capitalises on and Goetz revels in.

For a short song, now obscure, it sure had a lot of resonance when it was published.

In Warwick Deeping's 1913 novel *The White Gate*, the protagonist comes across a mysterious woman singing in her garden. The two songs, significantly, are "Pale Hands I Loved Beside the Shalimar" by Amy Woodforde-Finden and "Mélisande in the Wood" by Alma Goetz, both published eleven years earlier. He listens and reflects that the only kind of music he's ever enjoyed was from street organs, rampant marches and comic songs whose rhythms spoke of the "clatter of hammers". But suddenly:

> …he found himself in the humour to listen to more subtle utterances, recognising in them something essentially modern, a wounded self-consciousness, a sentimental and tired decadence. So that music had come to be too intimately expressive, moaning with him, and making him long for those strong, barbaric days when ordered sound was as the clangour of swords.[3]

Alma Goetz was Liza Lehmann's sister. Frustrated at the lack of information on her, I contacted Steuart Bedford, Lehmann's grandson and a conductor of some renown. He emailed: "I am not in the least surprised to hear that you cannot find any information about my great-aunt Alma; I am in the same boat having absolutely nothing to offer. Some years ago I picked up a short song published under her name but that is all I have to prove that she existed."

I was still finding references to "Mélisande in the Wood". Shortly after that email, I discovered this in a periodical published by the Egg Marketing Board of New South Wales in 1950: "There was to be a meeting in the local hall the other night over certain road matters. As it was long after the advertised starting time and the civic fathers hadn't turned up, someone suggested a 'sing-song'. One farmer's wife with a passable voice (when not rousing on Dad or the kids) was chosen to open the programme. The opening words of her ditty were apt: *Drink deep from the water, Mélisande.* The rising flood waters were lapping the back steps of the hall."[4] The unpredictability of the past. Only the most arthouse weirdo would choose that song for a farmer's wife in rural 1950s New South Wales. If it happened in a historical drama I would hurl things at the TV in disbelief.

But *Port of London Monthly* refers to the song as well. Speaking of the naming of boats on the "M system": "... Medea, Mentor, Morpheus, Medusa – might continue with the Melisande, though she ought not to pay attention to the line of the song 'Drink deep of the water, Melisande'."[5]

It was popular where the dockers lived in London. Clare Cameron's memoirs *Rustle of Spring: An Edwardian Childhood in London's East End* mention it, amongst evenings of music hall and "songs cut out of *The News of the World* and pasted onto brown paper". When her Uncle Jim brings some friends round "smelling of soap and hair-oil", they form a banjo and mandolin group, but disappoint her terribly because their upbeat minstrel ditties "didn't make one think of twisting little streets and dark casements, and moonlight". No, for that she had to go to Alma and Ethel's "Mélisande in the Wood" which she sight-reads in front of the assembled company: "What a strange and beautiful song! I sighed over the keys as the voice trailed soulfully away, and there was a respectful hush that follows something the company does not quite understand. Who was Mélisande, and what was she doing in the wood?"[6]

It even found its way into the South African wilds in a story by Florence Ethel Mills Young from 1911 called *Sam's Kid*. Two chums running a bone mill find themselves suddenly responsible for a young woman just out of school. After a few days of her

Alma Goetz's "Mélisande in the Wood" is barely two minutes long, for one singer and a piano, and yet it has mysterious depths, a presence like a ghost.

sitting around and making them uncomfortable, they buy her a piano. She reacts by "gazing down on the ivory keys with eyes that swam in tears".[7] She makes music for them as they sit and smoke on the step, moving them to a state of "ecstatic enjoyment." The romantic apotheosis of the book is when she sings and plays "Mélisande in the Wood": "It was a song Sam had never heard her sing before, and he thought as he listened to her that she might have been Mélisande, betrayed, deserted, despairing, wandering in the solitude of the silent wood."[8]

The other man brings her a deep red rose and, when the song ends, touches it to his lips, lays it against her face and then places it lightly next to her hands. Which results in a beautifully Edwardian sentence: "She looked at the blood-red petals on the ivory keys."[9]

Blood is there in *The White Gate,* where the protagonist reflects ever more extravagantly: "It was like the cry of the soul of the age, awed yet rebellious, conscious of faintness under the stars that shine in the blackness of an immense mystery. 'Drink deep, drink deep of the water Mélisande.' Why should he feel as though the blood of his soul was flowing out upon the grass? ... It seemed to him that he listened to one that was unhappy, and on the edge of revolting for the sake of self-expression."[10]

Interestingly, "Mélisande in the Wood" was the favourite song of the father of film-composer James Bernard[11], who wrote the scores for many Hammer Horror films, including *Taste the Blood of Dracula, The Secret of Blood Island, Frankenstein and the Monster from Hell,* and *She.*

Poet Ethel Clifford's parents were famous: her father was mathematician William Clifford, whose *On the Space Theory of Matter* anticipated Einstein's Theory of Relativity, and who died of overwork at 33. Her mother was author Lucy Lane Clifford, adored by Henry James, who said she was so like a gorgeous butterfly, he felt like a slug beside her. Lucy wrote *Mrs Keith's Crime* in 1885, a novel in a stream-of-consciousness form far ahead of its time, and also two ghoulishly nightmarish fairy tales, *The New Mother* and *Wooden Tony.* Mrs Clifford and her daughters were friends of Leslie Stephens, father of Vanessa (later Bell) and Virginia (later Woolf).

So often, the person I want to find out about is the one in the shadows. Sometimes they have famous offspring, sometimes, like Ethel, they have famous parents and friends, but they themselves just wrote "a few verses" or penned "a few songs". To find out about Ethel, I had to read Virginia and Vanessa's bitchy letters. According to Vanessa, Ethel "talked with a lisp and confided to me that her ambition in dress was to be able to throw a piece of lace carelessly over her shoulder so that the result should be perfection. Somehow in spite of this ideal and her Burne-Jones features, she could not help being like her mother, vulgar, rollicking Lucy Clifford"[12]. Virginia said of Ethel in 1927 that there was "something mincing, powdered, affected, vulgar, effusive, fawning" about her. "She wanted me to lunch with her and give a prize to a Frenchman." [13] A letter from Joseph Conrad paints a different picture. "We had a long talk ... She was charming, with something unconsciously

Poet Ethel Clifford, whose parents were mathematician William Clifford and bohemian Lucy Lane Clifford, who wrote in a stream-of-consciousness form.

mysterious in her charm. I remember also being appallingly stupid that evening." [14]

Ethel married Sir Fisher Wentworth Dilke, Baronet, in 1905. He also disapproved of his bride's literary, bohemian mother. Ethel stopped writing poems and her 1949 obituary said she was lost to poetry but would be remembered as "a gardener of genius".

Before her marriage, Ethel's poems provided precisely what restless, dream-heavy girls wanted. They were full of shadows, forests, knights, cups, waters, weeds and dusks. "Isuelt of Brittany", "The Ship of Dreams" and a "Desolate Princess" asking: "What shall it avail me making pools of water? Never more reflected shall I see his face. Root out from my borders calamus and camphire. All the earth henceforward is a desert place."[15]

I doubt many of the shrubs or bulbs of this "gardener of genius" survive, but some of her poetry does, tiny and behind glass; twenty-one of her poems are in the miniature volumes in Edwin Lutyens' 1921 doll house for Queen Mary in Windsor Castle.

These songs and poems are subtly different to the songs from this era written by men. I know it when I'm singing them. They are more sophisticated in some ways, less sophisticated in others. There are long pauses, shameless repetitions. Dame Ethel Smyth, composer of operas, symphonies, all the muscular forms, wrote in one of her fabulous memoirs that a woman is less conventional but also less haunted by a dread of being commonplace. "None of the few women composers who have contrived to get their songs printed are afraid of melody."[16] One could also say the poets aren't afraid of sentiment.

I noticed when playing through endless piles of sheet music that when I got to women's songs they *were* a little bit "too intimately expressive" and they *did* seem to moan with me, as Deeping said in 1913. Of all the major Christmas carol texts, it is Christina Rossetti's "In the Deep Midwinter" that is most personal and intimate with its "Breastful of milk" and "Yet what I can I give him; give my heart". The earnest sincerity in some of these songs by Victorian women can be off-putting to performers, and when they are performed, they don't play well if the sincerity isn't real. The parlour, with its velvet hush, its piano and needlepoint, was the place where men felt most self-conscious and out of their element. A woman wouldn't feel like that at all; she would lean back in the chintz or lean forward – depending on context – and ask about your troubles. Then she would tell of hers or brighten you up with a joke or a bit of gossip.

Alma Goetz's famous sister Liza Lehmann, who started composing after she quit her singing career, "became human, and married"[17], played by her own rules and composed the first Romantic-era English song cycle, *In a Persian Garden*. Having proved the doubters wrong by its roaring success, she composed others. Like Amy Woodforde-Finden, who was also posthumously featured in the music at the Indian Pavilion in the Exhibition at Wembley, she chose to set the verses of Sarojini Naidu, the *Bharatiya Kokila*, the "Nightingale of India".

"If I could write just one poem full of the spirit of beauty and greatness, I should be exultantly silent for ever; but I sing just as the birds do, and my songs are as ephemeral," Naidu wrote to Arthur Symons when he persuaded her to publish the anthology *The Golden Threshold*. One year later, Lehmann made a song cycle from it. The alto solo "Alabaster" *(CD track 32)* beautifully symbolises the secrecy and depth of female desire. Lehmann's music is headily exotic in the extreme; published in 1906, it was twenty years before this type of melody became almost universally associated with the sort of movie that starred the smouldering Rudolph Valentino.

Naidu must have liked the settings; she dedicated her poem 'The Dance of Love' to Lehmann:

The music sighs and slumbers,
It stirs and sleeps again...
Hush, it wakes and weeps and murmurs
Like a woman's heart in pain...[18]

While in England, Naidu was involved in women's suffrage. After the Amritsar Massacre in 1919, when peaceful protesters were trapped in the walled garden of Jallianwallah Bagh and British troops emptied 1,650 rounds of ammunition into them, Naidu stopped writing poetry and concentrated on politics, touring the world pleading for Indian independence, becoming president of the Indian National Congress and governor of United Provinces of Agra and Oudh.

In 1900 Lehmann wrote a set of songs for children called *The Daisy Chain*. My favourite is "If No-One Ever Marries Me" *(CD track 33)*, a comforting list of back-up plans devised by a Victorian girl already being threatened with the idea of spinsterhood. No problem, she reckons: she'll buy a squirrel in a cage, a little rabbit hutch, a pony, a clean and tame lamb, and when really old at twenty-eight she'll buy an orphan girl and "bring her up as mine". When I was the age the lyricist and composer had in mind, I thought it was silly to assume that every little girl will grow up with an inheritance of suitably vast proportions to put these plans into practice. Now, I find it sweet and realistically poignant. Why wouldn't the girl of a well-off family think the money would be forthcoming, at that age? And what a lovely way to want to spend it. Beats gold toilet seats and snakeskin-lined yachts. Despite its implied financial entitlement, I liked the song enormously as a child. It was an assertive characterisation of girlhood I hadn't seen

Laurence Alma-Tadema, who published a book on The Meaning of Happiness and spread her message on a lecture tour of America and around the UK.

elsewhere; a love of animals, proactive independence and a desire to help orphans.

The lyrics for "If No-One Ever Marries Me" were by Laurence Alma-Tadema, daughter of the painter Lawrence Alma-Tadema. In 1909, Laurence published a book on *The Meaning of Happiness* which took her on lecture tours to America and around the UK. She advocated independence and wrote that the yielding of the will is a wilful act, desire to be led is as vain as the desire to lead and that dependence impairs conscience. "We are meant to stand alone – the more we support, the more surely we weaken; the more we lean, the more heavily we fall." She also warned of the ever-widening expenditure of strength and means in modern life. "Opportunities to scatter our forces is growing year by year," she wrote exactly a century before the year Facebook tripled in size and Twitter went from four million to 40 million users. "The average life tends to be all foreground, like a badly-composed unsatisfying landscape."[19]

One of her volumes of poetry, *Songs of Womanhood*, contains a mixture of innocent verses about babies, birds and flowers, and gentle, deep anguish. "I've thrown my heart in a well, mother/For the lily was sick, and needed rain/O I've wept a cloud round my soul, mother/And we never shall see it again."[20]

When she lived in Wittersham, Kent, she built what she called a "Hall of Happy Hours" for the local children, writing plays and songs for them to perform and having them learn handicrafts. She filled it with handlooms and started a trend for homespun that resulted in textile exhibitions by The Romney Marsh Weavers in the 1920s. It seated about a hundred and was also known as St Luke's Hall so that it wouldn't be confused with St John's Church nearby. It is now St Luke's Cottage and has been converted into a private house. Laurence spent most of her money on refugees in the First World War and was secretary of the Polish Victims' Relief Fund. She had to sell the hall and her home, The Fair Haven, in 1925.

She never married and had no children of her own. Laurence died in 1940 in a nursing home in Chelsea.

In the years when women were just starting to be educated at music colleges, when *Lady's Pictorial* in 1885 made the jolly proclamation that the honorary doctor of music hat was "one of the most universally-becoming kinds of headgear", larger works by women started to be written and performed. My sheet music collection doesn't include these because, for one thing, many were never published. It is easy for me to sit down at a piano and play through a simple song, but to gather a choir, an orchestra and copy out the parts for them (even if one could get one's hands on the music in any form), to pay for their time and a hall – that is a challenge.

Looking at the mouth-watering lists of cantatas and symphonic poems is an almost surreal dream. These women didn't just write Masses in G and Requiems. Alice Mary Smith, 1839-84, wrote two concert overtures, *The Masque of Pandora* and *The Argonauts and the Sirens*, as well as cantatas *The Red King* and *Ode to the Northeast Wind* and an *Ode to the Passions*. Amy Elise Horrocks, 1867-1916, wrote *An Idyll of New Year's Eve* and *Undine* for orchestra as well as an 'orchestral ballade' *Romaunt of the Page*. Rosalind Ellicott, 1857-1924, wrote *Elysium* for solo soprano, chorus and orchestra and *Henry of Navarre*, a choral ballad with orchestra. Emily Lawrence, 1854-1894, wrote *The Ten Virgins* and *All Deep Things are Song* for women's voices. Mary Grant Carmichael, 1851-1935, wrote an operetta called *The Frozen Heart or The Snow Queen*. Frances Allitsen, 1848-1912, who had a picture of Kitchener in her music room for inspiration, wrote a *Slavonique Overture*. In America, prodigy Amy Beach, 1867-1944, whose astonishing ear was used by ornithologists to collect and notate birdsong before recording devices could adequately pick them up, wrote a cantata for female voices called *The Rose of Avontown*, *The Minstrel and the King* for male voices and, for mixed choir and orchestra, *Canticle of the Sun*, which I have heard – it's marvellous. Another American, Emma Steiner, 1856-1929, wrote operettas *The Viking*, *The Sleeping Beauty*, *The Alchemist* and *Fleurette* and also managed to found and run a home for elderly and infirm musicians. Suffrage campaigner Eleanor Smith, 1858-1942, wrote a cantata called *The Golden Asp* and an operetta entitled *Trolls' Holiday*. I could go on and on.

There seems a sense of fantasy, wonderment and shadowy dreamscapes waiting to be found. But perhaps in the inner sanctum, where the piano is kept, and further in, where the voice is kept, is one of the best ways to find this "revery," this something other, this extra.

The Use of it All

WHEN WE TAKE music lessons, we are often encouraged to picture ourselves as a soloist in evening dress or tuxedo, bowing on a vast stage amidst a storm of applause. If we don't end up being this person, we've fallen short of expectations.

For thirty years, I refused to think of myself as a pianist. I never played a concerto, I was too lazy – or unable – to give a Chopin recital to rival other Chopin recitals, and left piano to learn how to sing. But for the past fifteen years I have played the organ in a church and, for five years, have concurrently played piano in another church. In both I have been able to see that the person playing the instrument brings people together, enhances celebration and at a funeral, allows mourners to feel visceral support from others around them. To have seventy people heave a sigh of relief as you put your hands on the keys; knowing the difference you make as you see your fingers capably stretch out to make the chord that helps everyone feel better is worth all the childhood tantrums and hours of practise.

I was recently singing at a festival in Yorkshire and, over breakfast, discussed the history of music festivals with my host and festival volunteer Christina. This one had just won an award for outreach and artistic excellence and featured fabulous musicians that year from Sweden, Slovakia, Italy, Austria and Ireland. But when it started eighty years ago, it was a showcase for local musicians. As were most music festivals. They were where children wore their best clothes to perform recitations, where young people showed the songs they had been working on and where choirs shared the fruits of their constant rehearsals. Brass bands from neighbouring towns compared embouchure and tone, and cakes were baked to feed them all.

Were there any choirs in the village today? There was one, Christina told me. They used to meet, exchange news, talk of writing projects and local politics and sing. But the pianist now had arthritis and her fingers bent too far inward to play the notes.

"One of Ulster's best-known composers" Dorothy Parke was also a successful piano and violin teacher, introducing numerous children to the joys of musicianship.

There was no pianist to replace her. I asked if, maybe, a young person studying piano could be brought in? It would be a mutually beneficial arrangement; accompanying a choir flexes a whole new set of music muscles and forces one to keep going and be versatile in one's approach. She shook her head. Young people aren't learning the piano so much anymore.

Then I saw clearly what nobody had ever told me, like the sun bursting out over a dark mountain. There will *always* be people who can play Grieg piano concertos. There may be less music in schools, but we will never run out of violinists who can stand up in front of an orchestra and dazzle us with a cadenza, or showy pianists ready to set the grand's lid a-flapping with the force of their thundered repeated chords. Orchestras will always have many more people competing for positions than there are positions to fill. But the world desperately needs people to help in the creation of music around us, in our everyday lives.

Dorothy Parke, who wrote "The House and the Road", can be found in newspaper archives of the 1920s and 30s. Her listings are all to do with children taking exams. *The Derry Journal* of 1924 lists the Incorporated Society of Musicians' Local Centre Exams results: Isaac Kelly got distinction in grade 1 violin; while Norman Bell was granted honours in grade 1 piano. "Pupils of Miss Dorothy Parke," the paper announces proudly. Five years later, the same paper informs readers: "Miss Dorothy Parke resumes tuition in pianoforte, violin and all theoretical work." By 1954, young Mollie Dunlop is performing the songs of Parke, whom the *Lisburn Herald and Antrim and Down Advertiser* tells us is "now one of Ulster's best-known composers". *The New Grove Dictionary of Women Composers* records that she wrote "many songs and piano pieces that were used in music competitions … very approachable but of a rather naive simplicity".[1] And yet, that simplicity helped seed the nation with superheroes who have the power to bring people together so they can help one another and transform their interactions through music.

Imagine if only professional makeup artists were allowed to use foundation, eyeshadow brushes and lipstick, and we had to go to a salon to have it done? How much better a cake tastes when we've made it ourselves; when we can distinguish the flavours of ingredients we have personally mixed together. Hearing someone play Beethoven's *Für Elise* is pleasant, but when the notes are put together with your own hands, it becomes a continuously unfolding miracle. Music should be for us – ourselves and each other. We should all be able to have a go, even if it's using a pair of chopsticks to beat rhythms on a tin.

The women who wrote songs for us to sing at home provided a service beyond price. Nobody escapes sorrow, but to be able to sing or pick up an instrument can be a great solace. A piece of music written by someone who understands our needs, music that isn't forbiddingly difficult to perform, is a gift. Liza Lehmann's "Evensong" is an example *(CD track 34)*. She wrote it after the eldest of her two children died in training before being sent overseas in 1916. "Dear loving angels, pass not by, hush me to sleep". The text was written by Constance Morgan, whose poems were published by the *Westminster Gazette*. Lehmann's setting has a gentle fluttering in the piano that is like a soothing caress. She died shortly after, yet another of our women who died during a war.

Carrie Jacobs-Bond also knew tragedy in her personal life. Having started her music empire to provide for her son, she had the horrific news in 1920 that he had killed himself with a gunshot to the head; according to the sensationalistic reports, while listening to "A Perfect Day" on the gramophone. A cruel irony when that very song had prompted hundreds to write to the composer with stories of how singing it or hearing it gave them courage to press on during desperate times.

Caroline Sheridan Norton, who fought so hard for the right to have custody of her three boys, lived to see two die, and the last one on his deathbed. Her consoling poem "Not Lost, but Gone Before" is still to be found printed on funeral programmes, etched into jewellery and engraved onto headstones in graveyards the world over.

Who knows how many tragedies the songs these women wrote helped alleviate? How many girls had their lives galvanised by the energy and solidarity found in Mary Neal's Morris Dances? How much braver were the children in Norfolk's Charity Schools after Sarah Glover transformed their world into one of sung harmony?

I remember when museums used to display objects such as ancient bowls on transparent plexiglass plinths against a stark white background in the glare of cold, clinical spotlights. Though the object was beautiful, it was never designed to be looked at in this way. It was meant to be used; in the case of a bowl, to have olives in it and sit on a crisp linen cloth, bringing out the texture of the earth it was made from and the subtle depth of the weave of the dried flax fibres playing in the sun that moved families from one day to another. If the bowl had a wooden spoon in it, the evocation of living hands might even make us notice the fingerprints of the potter.

Museums are much more human nowadays and curators are careful to make things warmer, more approachable, more natural and sympathetic. They even put spoons in bowls. But what of concert halls? The Royal College of Music has collaborated with Imperial College to create a concert hall simulator to study the psychology of performance, and also for musicians to accustom themselves to the dry, alien moonscape that is the purpose-built modern performance venue. The uncomfortable hush, the black velvet sterility of the stage and the merciless lighting that reduces the people in the audience to shadowy, faceless figures are all clearly replicated. This isn't a place for comfort. I have always felt a kinship with Wanda Landowska, the harpsichordist whose career spanned 1900 to 1954, who insisted the stages she performed on be decorated with her own Persian rugs and shaded lamp. In many instances, she walked on stage barefoot to perform her beloved Bach.

There's a reason these domestic songs work so well at nursing homes: the audience is close by. Their need for music is intermingled with a need for human contact. When I start "Bless This House" at a nursing home, there's an intent silence that seems to lean in towards me. At the end, the audience members are either so enthusiastic they can't wait until the pianist finishes the last few bars and applaud while she's still playing, or they sit in magical hush for a few seconds after the last chord has died away, then exhale together as they clap as loud as delicate bones will allow.

Publishing scion Leslie Boosey said of May Brahe in an interview in 1967: "It was all tonic and dominant as they say but she and Helen Taylor had a direct simplicity which went straight to the hearts of the people."[2] Most artists will say that simplicity is the most difficult thing to get right, as master potter after master potter will try to replicate something as lovely as that ancient earthenware bowl. Claribel's songs may be so simple that she's been denied more than a small footnote in music history, but you can embody them at home. And try getting those tunes out of your head.

References

A SONG TO SING
1 Virginia Woolf, A Room of One's Own, p102 (London: The Hogarth Press, 1929)
2 The Musician, vol 18 p412 (Philadelphia: Hatch Music Company, 1913)

A VERY LARGE HOUSE
1 May Brahe, "Music", nd, copy held in the May Brahe biographical file of the Australian Dictionary of Biography, (Canberra: Australian National University)
2 Carl Sferrazza Anthony, America's First Families; An Inside View of 200 Years of Private Life in the White House. p16 (New York: Simon & Schuster, 2000)

CLARIBEL AND THE BEETHOVEN FILTER
1 Claribel (Charlotte Alington Barnard), Thoughts, Verses and Songs p177 (London: James Nisbet & Co, 1877)
2 Oskar Adolf Hermann Schmitz Das Land Ohne Musik – Englische Gesellschaftsprobleme (Munich: G. Müller, 1904)
3 Claribel (Charlotte Alington Barnard), Fireside Thoughts, Ballads, etc. etc. [sic] p141 (London: James Nisbet and co. 1865)
4 Phyllis Smith The Story of Claribel p120 (London: J.W. Ruddock & Sons, 1965)

THE FOLK SUFFRAGISTS
1 Ralph Vaughan-Williams "Lucy Broadwood 1858-1929" Journal of the English Folk Dance and Song Society (London: EFDSS, 1948)
2 Mary Neal The Espérance Morris Book p1 (London: J. Curwen & Sons 1910)
3 Ibid
4 Cecil Sharp p162 The New Age: A Weekly Review of Politics, Literature and Art vol 12 (London: New Age Press 1912)
5 EFDS News, No. 22, 1930

6 Rolf Gardiner p10 The Travelling Morrice and the Cambridge Morris Men Offprint
7 When I went back to the RVW Memorial Library they'd just had a refurbishment and I could not find the letter or pamphlet I wrote this down from. I looked for hours and on two additional occasions. It's very much in character for Rolf the Ranger, and you'll just have to take my word on it!
8 Folk Music Journal vol 5, issue 5 p575 (London: EFDSS, 1946)
9 Rolf Gardiner World Without End p39-40 (London: Corben-Sanderson 1932)
10 Josephine McGill "Following Music in a Mountain Land" Musical Quarterly No. 3, vol 3 (New York: Schirmer 1917)
11 Donald A. Precosky, "Marjorie Pickthall 1883-1922" Poetry Foundation Website
12 E.K. Brown On Canadian Poetry, p67 (Toronto: Ryerson 1943)
13 Lorne Pierce The Selected Poems of Marjorie Pickthall ¬introduction (Toronto: McClelland and Stewart 1957)
14 Tom Cook "Cecil Sharp and Mary Neal; Recollections by Douglas Kennedy as communicated to Tom Cook English Dance & Song April/May 1988 (London: EFDSS)
15 Sorley MacLean "On Realism in Gaelic Poetry" p87 Transactions of the Gaelic Society in Inverness, 1934-36 vol 37

CHILDREN, CHURCH, CHANGE
1 Louise Jury, Independent Newspaper, 12th October 1996
2 © Bernadette Farrell, OCP Publications, 1994
3 Sarah Glover Scheme for Rendering Psalmody Congregational, 1835; Together with the Sol-fa Tune Book, 1839 p8 (London: Boethius Press 1982)
4 ibid, p25

SONGS AS GIFTS
1 Robert MacAlarney "Preface" in Carrie Jacobs Bond The Roads of Melody (New York: D Appleton and Company 1927)

TWO IDENTITIES IN SOUTH LONDON
1 Avril Coleridge Taylor The Heritage of Samuel Coleridge Taylor p120 (London: Dennis Dobson, 1979)

2 G.R. Harvey Aberdeen Weekly Journal 15th May 1941 (Aberdeen: D.C. Thomson & Co. Inc)
3 Avril Coleridge Taylor The Heritage of Samuel Coleridge Taylor p133 (London: Dennis Dobson, 1979)
4 Stephen Bourne "Avril Coleridge Taylor: Daughter of Samuel Coleridge Taylor" p9-10 Black and Asian Studies Association Newsletter No. 46 November 2006

THE REFUGE AND REFORM OF CAROLINE SHERIDAN NORTON
1 Alan Chedzoy, A Scandalous Woman p141 (London: Allison & Busby, 1992)
2 Jane Grey Perkins, The Life of Mrs. Norton p297 (London: John Murray, 1910)
3 Karl Marx "The Duchess of Sutherland and Slavery" The People's Paper, No. 45 March 12, 1853
4 County Courts Chronicle, January to December, 1851 vol IV; Morgan Lloyd Ed. p114 (London: John Crockford, County Courts Chronicle office, 1852)

INDIA BY WAY OF A PARLOUR PIANO (AND THE NORTH CIRCULAR)
1 John Hullah, Music in the House p31 (London: Macmillan and Co. 1877)
2 Liza Lehmann The Life of Liza Lehmann p89 (London: T. Fisher Unwin 1919)
3 Carol Anderson ed. Violet Jacob Diaries and Letters from India 1895-1900 (London: Canongate 1990)
4 Laurence Hope (Violet Nicholson) "Men Should Be Judged" p62 Stars of the Desert (New York: John Lane 1903)
5 Laurence Hope (Violet Nicholson) "Last Poem" p50 (New York: John Lane 1905)

SOMETHING OTHER
1 Lorne Pierce: Introduction The Selected Poems of Marjorie Pickthall (Toronto: McClelland and Stewart 1957)
2 University of Toronto Quarterly vol 1 p358 (Toronto: University of Toronto Press 1931)
3 Warwick Deeping The White Gate p63 (New York: Robert M. McBride & Company 1911)
4 The Poultry Farmer vol 18 (Egg Marketing Board for the State

of New South Wales 1950)
5 Port of London Monthly vol 18 (1974)
6 Clare Cameron Rustle of Spring: An Edwardian Childhood in London's East End p67 (London: Skilton & Shaw 1979, originally published 1927)
7 Florence Ethel Mills Young Sam's Kid p90 (London: John Lane)
8 Ibid p306
9 Ibid p369
10 Warwick Deeping The White Gate p64 Ibid
11 David Huckvale James Bernard, Composer to Count Dracula: A Critical Biography p11 (Jefferson, North Carolina: 2006)
12 Vanessa Bell Sketches in Pen and Ink: A Bloomsbury Notebook ed. Lia Giachero p74-75 (London: The Hogarth Press 1997)
13 Virginia Woolf A Change of Perspective The Letters of Virginia Woolf vol. III 1923-28 Ed. Nigel Nicolson p349 (London: Hogarth Press 1977)
14 The Collected Letters of Joseph Conrad, vol 9 Uncollected Letters and Indexes Danes, Knowles, Moore & Stape ed. p266 (Cambridge: Cambridge University Press 2007)
15 Ethel Clifford Songs of Dreams p112 (London: John Lane 1903)
16 Ethel Smythe A Final Burning of Boats p13 (London: Longmans, Green and Co. Ltd. 1928)
17 Liza Lehmann The Life of Liza Lehmann p41 (London: T. Fisher Unwin 1919)
18 Sarojini Naidu, The Bird of Time Songs of Life, Death & the Spring p21 (London: William Heinemann 1912)
19 Laurence Alma-Tadema, The Meaning of Happiness p17-62 (London: Elkin Mathews 1909)
20 Laurence Alma-Tadema, "The Clouded Soul" Songs of Womanhood p46 (London: Grant Richards 1903)

THE USE OF IT ALL
1 The New Grove Dictionary of Women Composers Julie Anne Sadie and Rhian Samuel, ed. p362 (London: MacMillan 1994)
2 Letter from Leslie Boosey to Harold Morgan, 21st May, 1967

Bibliography

A Century of Ballads 1810-1910 – Harold Simpson 1910

A Change of Perspective, The Letters of Virginia Woolf 1977

A Final Burning of Boats, Etc. – Ethel Smyth, 1928

A Life of Song – Marjory Kennedy-Fraser 1929

A Memory Sketch or Personal Reminiscences of My Husband, Genius & Musician, Samuel Coleridge-Taylor – Jessie Fleetwood Coleridge Taylor 1943

A Scandalous Woman, the Story of Lady Caroline Norton – Alan Chedzoy 1993

A Very Great Profession: The Woman's Novel 1914-1939 – Nicola Beauman 1983

Aristocratic Women and the Literary Nation 1832-1867 – Muireann O'Cinneide 2008

As Bees in Honey Drown, Elbert Hubbard and the Roycrofters – Charles Franklin Hamilton 1973

Back to the Land: The Pastoral Impulse in Victorian England from 1880 to 1914 – Jan Marsh 1982

Ballad of the Gentlemen of England and Other Poems – Meta Orred 1908

Black Edwardians, Black People in Britain 1901-1914 – Jeffrey P. Green 1998

Black Mahler, the Samuel Coleridge-Taylor Story – Charles Elford 2008

Black Poppies: Britain's Black Community and the Great War – Stephen Bourne 2014

Campaigning for the Vote, Kate Parry Frye's Suffrage Diary ed. Elizabeth Crawford, 2013

Capturing the Ear of the Populace: May Brahe and the Domestic Song Market, 1912-1953 by Kay Dreyfus; One Hand on the Manuscript 1995

Checkers Magazine vol. 1 No 5 Jan 1949

City Folk, English Country Dance and the Politics of the Folk in Modern America – Daniel Walkowitz 2010

Evelyn Sharp, Rebel Woman 1869-1955 – Evelyn V. John 2009

Fairy Tales As They Are, As They Were, and as They Should Be – Evelyn Sharp 1889

Gardens in Sun and Shade – Minnie Aumonier 1920

Gothic (Re)Visions, Writing Women as Readers – Susan Wolstenholme 1993

Heritage Craft Schools and Hospitals, Chailey, 1903-1948, Being an Account of the Pioneer Work for Crippled Children – Grace Thyrza Hannam Kimmins 1948

I Love You Truly, A Biographical Novel Based on the Life of Carrie Jacobs-Bond – Max Morath, 2008

Indian Angles: English Verse in Colonial India from Jones to Tagore – Mary Ellis Gibson 2011

Ira Aldridge, the Negro Tragedian – Herbert Marshall 1958

Jean Ingelow, Victorian Poetess – Maureen Peters 1972

John Ruskin – Tim Hilton, 2002

Lady Dilke: A Biography – Betty Ellen Askwith 1969

Last Poems – Laurence Hope (Adela Florence Nicolson) 1905

Music in the House – John Hullah 1877

Musical Women in England 1870-1914 "Encroaching on All Man's Privileges" – Paula Gillett 2000

Negro Musicians and their Music – Maud Cuney Hare 1996

New Found Voices, Women in Nineteenth Century English Music – Derek Hyde 1984

Perils of he Night: A Feminist Study of 19th Century Gothic – Eugenia C. DeLamotte 1990

Radical Writing on Women, 1800-1850, An Anthology – Kathryn Gleadle 2002

Resonances of the Raj, India in the English Musical Imagination 1897-1947 – Nalini Ghuman

Rustle of Spring, An Edwardian Childhood in London's East End – Clare Cameron 1979

Sam's Kid – Florence Ethel Mills Young 1911

Samuel Coleridge Taylor, Anglo-Black Composer 1875-1912 (2nd Edition) – William Tortolano 2003

Samuel Coleridge-Taylor, Musician: His Life & Letters – W. C. Berwick Sayers 1915

Sarojini Naidu: An Introduction to her Life, Work and Poetry – Vishwanath S. Naravane 1980

Sarojini Naidu: Her Way With Words – Mushirul Hasan 2012

Scheme for Rendering Psalmody Congregational – Sarah Glover 1835

Sketches in Pen and Ink: A Bloomsbury Notebook – Vanessa Bell 1997

Songs of Dreams – Ethel Clifford 1903

Songs of Womanhood – Laurence Alma-Tadema 1903

Stars of the Desert – Laurence Hope (Adela Florence Nicolson) 1903

Such Silver Currents, the Story of William and Lucy Clifford, 1845-1929 – Monty Chisholm 2002

The Adventurous Thirties: A Chapter in the Women's Movement – Janet Elizabeth Courtney 1933

The Amazing Story of the Floral Dance – Ian Marshall 2003

The Arts and the American Home, 1900-1930 – ed Jessica Foy, Karal Ann Marling 1994

The Chautauqua Moment; Protestants, Progressives, and the Culture of Modern Liberalism, 1874-1920 – Andrew Chamberlin Reiser 2003

The Collected Poems of Josephine Preston Peabody 1927

The Criminal Conversation of Mrs. Norton – Diane Atkinson 2013

The Diary and Letters of Josephine Preston Peabody 1911

The Esperance Morris Book – Mary Neal 1912

The Feminist Avant-Garde, Transatlantic Encounters of the Early 20th Century (Ideas in Context) – Lucy Delap 2007

The Golden Threshold – Sarojini Naidu 1905

The Heritage of Samuel Coleridge-Taylor – Avril Coleridge Taylor 1979

The Imagined Village: Culture, Ideology & the English Folk Revival – Georgina Boyes 2010

The Masochistic Pleasures of Sentimental Literature – Marianne Noble 2007

The Meaning of Happiness, A Discourse – Laurence Alma-Tadema 1909

The Narratives of Caroline Norton – Randall Craig 2009

The Pandora Guide to Women Composers, Britain and the United States, 1629-Present – Sophie Fuller 1995

The Roads of Melody – Carrie Jacobs-Bond 1927

The Singing Leaves: A Book of Songs and Spells – Josephine Preston Peabody 1903

The Song of a Tramp – Constance Morgan 1911

The White Gate – Warwick Deeping 1913

The White House Music Book – 1902

Thoughts, Verses and Songs – Claribel (Charlotte Alington Barnard) 1877

Trials of an Heiress – Mary Ann Danet Gifford 1869

Unfinished Adventure, Selected Reminiscences from an Englishwoman's Life – Evelyn Sharp 1933

Woman's Work in Music – Arthur Elson 1903

Women and the Settlement Movement – Katharine Beaumann 1996

Women Composers, the Lost Tradition Found – Diane Jezic 1988

Women of the Raj, The Mothers, Wives, and Daughters of the British Empire in India – Margaret Macmillan 2007

World Without End: British Politics and the Younger Generation – Henry Rolf Gardiner 1932

The British Newspaper Archive

Magazines, fragments, scans, clippings, interviews and of course, sheet music

It is highly recommended that this book is read in conjunction with its 34-track companion CD *She Wrote the Songs* (Songophile SONG51) from patriciahammond.com, where free audio samples are also available.

TRACKS
1. The House and the Road (music Dorothy Parke 1904-1990; words Josephine Preston Peabody 1874-1922)
2. Bless This House (music May Brahe 1884-1956; words Helen Taylor 1873-1943)
3. The Wide Brown Land (music May Brahe; words by Dorothea MacKellar 1885-1968)
4. Come Back to Erin (music and words Charlotte Alington Barnard "Claribel" 1830-1869)
5. Take Back the Heart (music Charlotte Alington Barnard; words Mary Ann Danet Gifford ?-1871)
6. Out on the Rocks (music Charlotte Sainton Dolby 1821-1885; words Charlotte Alington Barnard)
7. Duna (music Josephine McGill 1877-1919; words Marjorie Pickthall 1883-1922)
8. Chop Waltz (music by Euphemia Allan 1861-1948)

9   In the Gloaming (music Annie Fortescue Harrison 1848-1944; words Meta Orred 1845-1925)
10 A Perfect Day (music and words by Carrie Jacobs-Bond 1862-1946)
11-22 Half Minute Songs (music and words Carrie Jacobs-Bond)
23 When the Coloured Lady Saunters Down the Street (music and words Amanda Ira Aldridge 1866-1956)
24 Can Sorrow Find Me (music Avril Coleridge-Taylor 1903-1998; words Minnie Aumonier 1865-1952)
25 Juanita (music and words Caroline Sheridan Norton 1808-1877)
26 Forget Me Not (music and words Caroline Sheridan Norton)
27-30 Four Indian Love Lyrics (music Amy Woodforde-Finden 1860-1919; words Adela Florence Nicolson "Laurence Hope" 1865-1904)
31 Melisande in the Wood (music Alma Goetz 1868-?; words Ethel Clifford 1876-1959)
32 Alabaster, from The Golden Threshold (music Liza Lehmann 1862-1918; words Sarojini Naidu 1879-1949)
33 If No-One Ever Marries Me (music Liza Lehmann; words Laurence Alma-Tadema 1865-1940)
34 Evensong (music Liza Lehmann; words Constance Morgan)